Lonely
People

Other titles by Warren W. Wiersbe

Living Lessons
FROM GOD'S WORD

Lonely People

Biblical Lessons on Understanding
and *Overcoming* Loneliness

Warren W. Wiersbe

BakerBooks

A Division of Baker Book House Co
Grand Rapids, Michigan 49516

© 2002 by Warren W. Wiersbe

Published by Baker Books
a division of Baker Book House Company
P.O. Box 6287, Grand Rapids, MI 49516-6287

Previously published in 1983 by the Good News Broadcasting Association, Inc.

Printed in the United States of America

Library of Congress Cataloging-in-Publication Data

Wiersbe, Warren W.
    Lonely people : biblical lessons on understanding and overcoming loneliness / Warren W. Wiersbe.
        p.   cm. — (Living lessons from God's word)
    ISBN 0-8010-6399-X
    1. Loneliness—Religious aspects—Christianity. 2. Loneliness—Biblical teaching. I. Title. II. Series.
    BV4911 .W54 2002
    248.8′6—dc21   2002002315

For current information about all releases from Baker Book House, visit our web site:

http://www.bakerbooks.com

Contents

104 46

Preface

This book contains edited and expanded transcriptions of radio messages I delivered over the Back to the Bible international network. The last three chapters were written especially for this book.

These messages were first spoken to a listening audience made up of a variety of people in many nations and at many stages of spiritual growth. This explains the brevity, simplicity, and directness of the material. Were I writing a commentary or presenting a longer pulpit message, the approach would be vastly different.

In sending out these messages, my prayer is that they will encourage and build up God's people and help them in their own ministries.

Warren W. Wiersbe

The Meaning of Loneliness

Alone, alone, all, all alone,
Alone on a wide wide sea!
And never a saint took pity on
My soul in agony.

So wrote Samuel Taylor Coleridge in 1798 in "The Rime of the Ancient Mariner," a poem you probably had to read when you were in high school or college. He also wrote in that poem:

. . . This soul hath been
Alone on a wide wide sea:
So lonely 'twas, that God himself
Scarce seemed there to be.

Have you ever felt like that? Or have you ever tried to help somebody who felt that way? Loneliness isn't a new problem, is it? Loneliness has been with us a long, long time.

The psalmist wrote in Psalm 102:

Hear my prayer, O LORD; let my cry for help come to you. Do not hide your face from me when I am in distress. Turn your ear to me; when I call, answer me quickly. For my days vanish like smoke; my bones burn like glowing embers. My heart is blighted and withered like grass; I forget to eat my food. Because of my loud groaning I am reduced to skin and bones. I am like a desert owl, like an owl among the ruins. I lie awake; I have become like a bird alone on a roof.

verses 1–7

Perhaps you can identify with the psalmist in his loneliness. In a world experiencing a population explosion, it seems strange that loneliness is one of our greatest problems. Loneliness is something we must not overlook, because loneliness is serious.

The Consequences of Loneliness

Loneliness has physical consequences. It's interesting to note one survey that reported more than 50 percent of the heart patients studied confessed they were lonely and depressed before they had their heart attack. Some research even indicates a relationship between loneliness and certain kinds of cancer.

Loneliness also has emotional consequences. I found one study in which 80 percent of the psychiatric patients interviewed said they sought help because of their loneliness. Loneliness can lead people to become nervous, to overeat, to drink heavily, and to experience insomnia. Half a million people attempt suicide in the United States every year, and many of these attempts are linked to loneliness. People feel lonely day after day and decide to destroy themselves. At the Suicide Prevention Center in Los Angeles, California, many of the teenagers interviewed confessed that their suicide attempts started with feelings of loneliness.

Yes, loneliness has physical and emotional consequences, but it also has spiritual consequences. You see, God made us not to be lonely but to have fellowship with Him and with

10

the people around us. He made us to enjoy creative lives, to be people who are growing and enjoying the enrichment He provides. It's a sad thing when people are lonely and fail to achieve all that God wants them to achieve in their lives.

As we consider the meaning of loneliness, let's try to answer three very important questions: What is loneliness? What causes loneliness? Is there a cure for loneliness?

A Definition of Loneliness

What is loneliness? It's probably easier to *feel* than to describe. Professional people have their clinical definitions and common people have their personal ideas; but whether we read a psychology book or examine our own hearts, loneliness is nothing to joke about or to push aside lightly. A lonely teenager may be "going through a phase" or may be desperately in need of help. The same is true for a lonely senior citizen.

Loneliness means feeling like you're all by yourself when you're surrounded by all kinds of people, some of whom might want to meet you and chat with you. Loneliness is feeling emotional isolation even in a crowd; it is a feeling of being unwanted and unneeded. Lonely people get to the place where they automatically build walls instead of bridges and step back when others step forward to greet them. Lonely people face each day as if there's nothing to live for. Nobody really cares anymore. Loneliness eats away at the inner person until all emotional strength is sapped and hope is destroyed.

What Loneliness Is Not

We must distinguish between loneliness and solitude. Solitude is physical isolation, which can be good for us. Our Lord Jesus used to go out by Himself to meditate and to pray.

At one time, the apostle Paul left his friends so he could walk and meditate while they traveled by ship. He wanted solitude. He wanted to be alone.

In my own life, I find that every day I must go off by myself to think, to meditate, and to pray. I need to have my inner man "ventilated," as it were. The Word of God tells us it's good to be alone with God, to face yourself in the mirror of His Word, to meditate, to think, and to pray. People who always have to be busy are often trying to escape the realities of life.

We should note that being lonely is not the same as being lonesome. All of us have had the experience of being lonesome. In my own travels, when I've been away from my family, I've had the temporary feeling of being lonesome. But when you're lonesome, you know it's going to end. You're going to hop on a plane or get into an automobile or train and head for home. Our friends and loved ones who are away from home will one day return to us. Being lonesome is not as painful as being lonely.

Sometimes we have the feeling of being forlorn. Being forlorn is being lonesome plus experiencing grief and sadness. Often we're forlorn when we lose a loved one. We know we won't see that person again until we get to heaven, provided he or she was born again through faith in Jesus Christ.

What Loneliness Is

No, loneliness is not the same as solitude, lonesomeness, or forlornness. Loneliness is an inner feeling of isolation and insulation, when a person feels unwanted, unneeded, and unnecessary. As one comic put it, you feel like volunteering to be a speed bump! But no matter how much lonely people smile or tell you they're feeling fine, they are hurting inside.

I've pastored three churches, each of them in a metropolitan area, and I've noticed that the presence of many people is no protection against loneliness. In fact, crowds can make the feeling worse. When lonely people walk the city streets or go into a restaurant or a park and see other people having a good time with friends and family, it makes their own pain that much greater. Just as sick people sometimes feel worse when they see healthy people enjoying themselves, so lonely people withdraw when confronted by people who are enjoying life.

People who feel lonely often think about suicide during the holidays—especially Thanksgiving, Christmas, and Easter. These are times when people who have families and friends are rejoicing together. Lonely people feel terribly devastated during these holidays because they can't experience the joy that comes so easily to others.

Let me give you my own definition of loneliness: Loneliness is the malnutrition of the soul that comes from living on substitutes. That's what Isaiah 55 is talking about:

> Come, all you who are thirsty, come to the waters; and you who have no money; come, buy and eat! Come, buy wine and milk without money and without cost. Why spend money on what is not bread, and your labor on what does not satisfy? Listen, listen to me, and eat what is good, and your soul will delight in the richest of fare.
>
> Isaiah 55:1–2

Many lonely people are feeding their inner persons with substitutes. They're spending money for that which is not bread and laboring for that which does not satisfy. God offers them something worthwhile, something to satisfy and nourish the inner person, and He offers it "without money and without cost" (v. 1). That's the unbounded, unlimited grace of God.

People today have the idea that if you have a job, money, and food, you'll be satisfied. Yet Isaiah was saying, in effect, "You spend your money, but you aren't buying bread. You're laboring hard, but your work doesn't satisfy you. Yes, you're feeding the body and the pocketbook, but the inner person is starving and bankrupt. You're living on substitutes!"

Loneliness is the malnutrition of the soul that comes from living on substitutes. And the sad thing is, many of the people I meet are satisfied with substitutes. They're satisfied with entertainment when God offers them joy. They're satisfied with taking a sleeping pill when God offers them peace. They're satisfied with prices when God offers them values. They're satisfied with fun when God offers them abundant life. They're satisfied with playing a role in society when God wants to make them His own unique children.

The Causes of Loneliness

What causes loneliness? Sociologists, psychologists, and medical experts have been studying loneliness for many years. These specialists don't always agree, but they have come to some conclusions that help point the way to a better understanding of this modern malady.

Social Causes

The mobility of modern life leaves many people rootless. They have many casual acquaintances but very few deep and lasting friendships. How many people who live on your street or in your apartment building do you know personally? How many people who work in your office do you know? How many of them do you *want* to know? In the United States, an average of 20 percent of the population relocates every year. This means digging up their roots and

14

being transplanted, having to make new friends and find new doctors, dentists, barbers, hairdressers, grocery stores, and places of worship. But many people don't cultivate new friends that quickly, and they pay the price of mobility with loneliness.

I think the competitiveness of life also contributes to loneliness. We're busy succeeding and taking care of number one. We're so focused on ourselves that we forget about other people. The competition of life forces people *from* us instead of drawing people *to* us.

Some people are lonely because of fear. Real dangers exist in both big cities and small towns. Elderly people are afraid of being attacked. People who live in apartments have double and triple locks on their doors. They're afraid to speak to strangers, and perhaps you can't blame them.

You mix the mobility and competitiveness of modern life with fear and the fact that we live in a very impersonal society, and you can easily understand why so many people are lonely. When you go to the bank, you aren't a name, you're a number. When you go to a store, you're a credit card. People don't know our faces, and they don't remember our names. Yes, there are social causes of loneliness.

Psychological Causes

Loneliness also has psychological causes. I've noticed in my own pastoral ministry that lonely people often have similar characteristics. For one thing, they are hurt easily and their wounds don't heal quickly. Somewhere in life they've been deeply wounded and this has left them keeping their distance. Perhaps they've been turned down by a potential employer. Maybe they have been rejected by a friend or significant other. Whatever the circumstances, they hurt inside. They're afraid of being hurt again so they pull into their

15

protective shells. They carry inner wounds that fester until they experience the cleansing of God's grace and love.

Lonely people are not just hurting people; sometimes they're also guilty people. They may have a soiled conscience, or they may carry regrets from past mistakes and sins. Perhaps they've been sinned against and the stains are still there. Little do we realize the kind of baggage some people carry through life, baggage that needs to be taken to Jesus and left at the cross.

Lonely people are often insecure people. It takes a sense of personal security to be able to reach out to others and share yourself with them. You have to know where you stand and who you are and what you can do to be able to receive others and develop friendships. To most people, meeting others is a treat; but to lonely people, meeting others is a threat. You can't build strong relationships on insecure foundations.

Lonely people are sometimes confused people. They aren't sure who they are or where they're going or why they're here. That's why knowing God through faith in Jesus Christ starts us on the road to fulfillment, for when you know God, you know where you came from, who you are, and what God wants you to be and do.

Sometimes lonely people are selfish people whose lives are controlled by self-pity. They feel sorry for themselves, and they envy others who have more than they have and can do more than they can. Instead of being thankful for what they do have, they sit around feeling sorry for themselves because of what they don't have.

Spiritual Causes

I really believe that one of the root causes of loneliness is spiritual. Spiritual relationships are the most important

16

relationships in life. Life is built on relationships—your relationship to yourself, to others, to the creation around you, and most of all, to God. Being able to know yourself, accept yourself, and be yourself enables you to relate to others. I have learned that when my relationship to God, myself, and others is what it ought to be, loneliness is not a problem. When we leave God out of our lives or deliberately disobey Him, we open the way for loneliness to come in.

The Cure for Loneliness

Is there a cure for loneliness? Yes, there is. We can't easily change society, and we can't force others to change. Some lonely people may need professional Christian counseling. If your loneliness is bordering on depression and destruction, then you ought to get professional help from a competent Christian counselor. But lonely people can begin to experience inner healing by trusting Jesus Christ. He can restore broken relationships—with God, with ourselves, with creation, and with others. Jesus Christ can help us to know ourselves, accept ourselves, and be ourselves. Only Jesus Christ can cleanse us from the guilt of sin and give us an exciting new future. Only Jesus Christ can make us new people and give us the inner power to face life and handle its demands.

While loneliness may have social causes, loneliness is basically an inside problem. What life does to us largely depends on what life finds in us. The heart of every problem is the problem in the heart. That's why Jesus says, "Come to me, all you who are weary and burdened, and I will give you rest" (Matt. 11:28). Jesus Christ wants to move into your life and get acquainted with you and have you get acquainted with Him. He wants to cleanse you and make you a new person.

17

Together you and He can solve the problems that have been causing loneliness in your life.

Is there a cure for loneliness? Jesus Christ is the only one I know who can give you eternal and abundant life. That's why He came and lived and died, and today He lives to become your Savior, Lord, and friend. "The LORD is my shepherd, I shall not want" (Ps. 23:1 KJV).

2

Cain
THE LONELINESS OF SIN

We all know that Cain killed Abel, but did you know that Cain also killed Cain? Cain committed spiritual suicide and brought upon himself a life of loneliness and aimless wandering.

Life consists of living relationships. If I may use a simple image, life is made up of open doors, the most important of which is the open door to God that comes through faith in Christ. When you trust the Lord Jesus Christ, He opens the doors for you to enjoy a wonderful life of fulfillment.

Along with an open door to God, Jesus gives you an open door to other people—your family and friends, the people around you, and the family of God around the world. He also gives you an open door to yourself so that you can know yourself better, learn to accept yourself and live with yourself, and be able to use what God has given you for His glory. Finally, Jesus gives you an open door to the world around you, to life in God's great creation. He enables you to enjoy the beauties of nature and the blessings that God has put into this wonderful world.

The tragedy of Cain's life was that he closed all the doors. The story is found in Genesis 4. Cain and his brother Abel came to the altar of the Lord and each offered a sacrifice. The tragedy is that Cain offered the wrong sacrifice with the wrong attitude. He didn't bring a sacrifice of faith but one that represented his own hard work. By faith, Abel brought a sacrifice of blood, and God accepted him; but the Lord rejected Cain and his sacrifice, and this made Cain angry.

"Then the LORD said to Cain, 'Why are you angry? Why is your face downcast? If you do what is right, will you not be accepted? But if you do not do what is right, sin is crouching at your door; it desires to have you, but you must master it'" (Gen. 4:6–8). God talked to Cain about the doors in his life and warned him that sin was crouching like an animal at the door of his heart. If Cain opened that door and yielded to temptation, it would spring on him and destroy him. Sad to say, that's exactly what Cain did. Cain went out into the field and killed his brother.

> Then the LORD said to Cain, "Where is your brother Abel?" "I don't know," he replied. "Am I my brother's keeper?" The LORD said, "What have you done? Listen! Your brother's blood cries out to me from the ground. Now you are under a curse and driven from the ground, which opened its mouth to receive your brother's blood from your hand. When you work the ground, it will no longer yield its crops for you. You will be a restless wanderer on the earth." Cain said to the LORD, "My punishment is more than I can bear."
>
> Genesis 4:8–13

It's too bad Cain didn't say, "My sin is greater than I can bear!" But he wasn't really convicted about his sin; he was only concerned about the consequences. He could have asked for forgiveness, but instead he asked for protection. "Today you are driving me from the land, and I will be hidden from your presence; I will be a restless wanderer on the earth, and whoever finds me will kill me" (v. 14). God marked Cain in some special way so that nobody would kill him, but Cain's life was a living death apart from the blessing of the Lord. He had God's protection but not God's presence.

"So Cain went out from the LORD's presence" (v. 16). He lived in the land of Nod, which means "wandering," located east of Eden. There Cain built a city, and when you read about this civilization in Genesis 4:16–24, you find it was a great deal like our civilization today.

The problem that Cain had, of course, was the problem of closing the doors. He was a lonely man. He was a fugitive and a wanderer, not a pilgrim and a stranger. Those who have trusted Christ as Savior are pilgrims and strangers in this world. This world is not our home; heaven is our home, and our citizenship is there (Phil. 3:20). But there's a vast difference between being a pilgrim and a stranger and being a fugitive and a wanderer. The pilgrim knows where he is going and how he's going to get there. The fugitive—the wanderer—is looking for some destination, some quiet haven, where he can be safe and satisfied. How sad it is that Cain rejected the grace of God!

Let's notice the doors that Cain closed in his life and how closing those doors made him a lonely man.

Cain's Unbelief

First, Cain closed the door on God by his unbelief. God had taught Adam and Eve, and they had taught their sons, that God's way is the way of faith. "So then faith comes by hearing, and hearing by the word of God" (Rom. 10:17 NKJV). God had taught Adam and Eve the meaning of blood sacrifice. When God clothed them after their disobedience,

21

He killed innocent animals and used the skins to cover their nakedness (Gen. 3:21).

Cain knew this truth and so did Abel. When Abel came to the altar, he brought the firstborn of his flock. He brought the very best he had, and he brought it as an act of faith. Cain came with the produce of his field, and he came in unbelief. The Bible calls this "the way of Cain" (Jude 11). Cain was religious and no doubt sincere, but he was rejected by the Lord. Cain wanted his own way—the way of human effort, the way of human merit—not the way of faith; and Cain closed the door on God by his unbelief.

Have you done that? Have you really trusted Jesus Christ as your Savior? You say, "Well, there are so many things about God I don't understand." Welcome to the club! I've been a Christian for over half a century, and the longer I walk with God, the more mysterious some things become, but the more wonderful they become. It is such a blessed experience to walk with the Lord, to have the door of your heart opened to Him and to be in fellowship with God. That's the first step toward conquering loneliness—opening the door to God, getting right with Him, and having your sins forgiven through faith in Jesus Christ. "Everyone who calls on the name of the Lord will be saved" (Acts 2:21).

Cain's Hatred

Cain closed the door on God by his unbelief. But he closed a second door, and this made his loneliness even worse: He closed the door on his brother by his hatred. Some passages in 1 John help us understand what was wrong with Cain.

> Anyone who claims to be in the light but hates his brother is still in the darkness. Whoever loves his brother lives in the light, and there is nothing in him to make him stumble. But

whoever hates his brother is in the darkness and walks around in the darkness; he does not know where he is going, because the darkness has blinded him.

1 John 2:9–11

We can now understand how Cain became a fugitive and a wanderer: he hated his brother, and that hatred created darkness in his soul.

This is how we know who the children of God are and who the children of the devil are: Anyone who does not do what is right is not a child of God; nor is anyone who does not love his brother. This is the message you heard from the beginning: We should love one another. Do not be like Cain, who belonged to the evil one and murdered his brother. And why did he murder him? Because his own actions were evil and his brother's were righteous.

1 John 3:10–12

The Word of God makes it clear that hatred closes the door between us and other people. If we have hatred in our hearts toward a brother or if we're holding a grudge against somebody, it cuts us off from people and makes us feel lonely. Don't make the same mistake that Cain made. Cain closed the door on God through unbelief, and he closed the door on his brother through hatred.

You dare not separate these two. According to the great commandment (Matt. 22:34–40), we are to love God and also to love our neighbor. You can't say, "Well, my heart is open to God and I love God, but I hate my neighbor." The Word of God makes it very clear that love for God results in love for my brother. "If anyone says, 'I love God,' yet hates his brother, he is a liar. For anyone who does not love his brother, whom he has seen, cannot love God, whom he has not seen" (1 John 4:20).

Notice the stages in Cain's decision to close the door on his brother. First, he envied his brother. God showed respect to Abel and his offering, but He did not show respect to Cain and his offering. Cain was envious because his brother's sacrifice pleased God and was accepted. Cain's envy grew into anger and hatred and then a desire for revenge. Jesus said that hatred in the heart is the moral equivalent of murder (see Matt. 5:22).

The next step was hypocrisy. Cain lied to God about the sinful attitude in his heart. Cain went out into the field to talk to his brother, but he was really hiding his true intentions. Out in the field, he murdered his brother, and that closed the door.

Love always keeps the doors open. When you have a right relationship with God by faith, you will have a right relationship with your brother because of God's love in your heart. That means you will forgive others and be kind to them. "Be kind and compassionate to one another, forgiving each other, just as in Christ God forgave you" (Eph. 4:32).

Cain's Dishonesty

By his unbelief, Cain closed the door of his life on God, and by his hatred, he closed the door on his brother. Then he closed the door on himself by his dishonesty.

Unless you want to live in a world of illusion, you have to live with yourself and take responsibility for what you do. To live in denial is not to live at all, because you are closing doors all around you. "Then the LORD said to Cain, 'Where is your brother, Abel?' 'I don't know,' he replied. 'Am I my brother's keeper?'" (Gen. 4:9). Cain deliberately lied to the Lord; he did know where his brother's corpse was lying. Like Satan, Cain was both a liar and a murderer (John 8:44), and this made him a child of the devil (1 John 3:12). He closed the door on himself by his dishonesty and he spent the rest of his life bearing the consequences of his deception.

There is a great need today for integrity. Integrity means wholeness of the inner person. It is being honest with yourself and telling the truth to yourself and others. Shakespeare said in *Hamlet,* "To thine own self be true." Integrity is an important part of life, especially of the Christian life. The Lord Jesus said we shouldn't practice duplicity and have a double outlook on life. "The eye is the lamp of the body. If your eyes are good [single], your whole body will be full of light" (Matt. 6:22). But if your outlook is double—if you are looking at God with one eye and at the world with the other—then you will not have integrity. Your life will be characterized by duplicity and hypocrisy.

Cain closed the door on himself by his dishonesty, and in so doing, he lost his integrity. He was no longer a whole person. I wonder: Are you being dishonest with yourself? Perhaps you blame other people for what's happened to you. Maybe you blame God for what's happened to you. Have you ever thought of looking into the mirror and saying, "There is the problem"?

Repentance involves honesty. When people repent, they must be honest with themselves and with God. True repentance means saying, "I am the culprit! I am the one who is to blame!" Are you blaming your brother or sister for that family problem? Are you blaming the boss or your fellow workers for that difficulty in the office or in the shop? If you look in the mirror, you may discover the real culprit.

Cain's Despair and Loneliness

Finally, Cain closed the door on life itself by his despair and his loneliness. He said, "My punishment is more than I can bear" (Gen. 4:13). Why didn't he confess his sin? Why didn't he trust the grace of God? Instead, he began to blame God. "Today you are driving me from the land" (v. 14).

If you are not in a right relationship with the Creator, you won't be in a right relationship with His creation. We sing in one of our songs, "This is my Father's world." When you know God as your Father, then His world becomes a place where you can enjoy and serve Him. But if you don't know Him, if you've closed the door on Him, then this world becomes a prison. It becomes a concentration camp. No matter where you turn, you will find no satisfaction. You have closed the door on life itself by your despair.

"I'm a wanderer!" cried Cain. "I'm a fugitive!" What did Cain do to try to solve his problem? Cain desperately tried to conquer his loneliness by building a city. Cain had been a farmer, but now he built a city. Then he introduced the manufacture of various tools and weapons from bronze and iron. Cain started what we call human civilization.

Our present civilization is the consequence of what Cain did. We're back to human effort again. Cain's message was, "We can work and be satisfied. We can build culture. We will have tents and cattle, yes, but we will also have music, and we will have things made of iron and bronze. We will have craftsmen make artistic things for us." Culture is a fine thing if it glorifies God, but it is a tragic substitute if God is left out.

We find in Cain's civilization the breakdown of the home. Lamech had two wives. God's standards for marriage were rejected. Cain tried to build culture without God. He tried to get a crowd around him and have activities that would distract him from the loneliness of sin. What happened? Did it solve the problem? No!

American naturalist Henry David Thoreau defined a city as a place where hundreds of people are lonely together. I have pastored in the city. I have walked the streets of the city, and I have seen the lonely faces there. It all started with Cain. He built for himself a hell on earth, but he thought it was a heaven on earth. His city had things and activities but no satisfaction, no salvation. He lived in the midst of a prison, and he thought he was having a wonderful time without God.

Cain speaks to us today about the tragic loneliness of sin. Sin is at the root of much loneliness. I'm not saying that everybody who is lonely is a terrible sinner like Cain, because sometimes loneliness stems from other experiences. But many people need to admit they have closed the door on God by their unbelief. They have closed the door on their brother by their hatred. They have closed the door on themselves by their dishonesty. Consequently, they have closed the door on the world and on life around them because of their despair and lack of sincere repentance. They are living on substitutes.

May I remind you of my definition of loneliness? Loneliness is the malnutrition of the soul that results from living on substitutes. Cain built a great civilization. The people in his city had opportunity and culture. They enjoyed science and even technology. But Cain was still a fugitive and a wanderer on the earth. Cain lived in the loneliness of sin.

The Lord Jesus Christ invites you to come and receive salvation: "I have come that they may have life," He said, "and have it to the full" (John 10:10). If you want real life to the full, open your heart to Him!

3

Job
THE LONELINESS OF SUFFERING

Except for our Lord Jesus Christ, probably no person in Scripture suffered as much as Job did. In one day, Job lost all of his wealth and all ten of his children. Then he lost his health. He lost the love of his wife, who suggested that he curse God and commit suicide. He lost the compassion of his friends. But he never really lost his faith in God. In the Book of Job we are introduced to a man who knew how to suffer.

Job said, "I despise my life; I would not live forever. Let me alone; my days have no meaning" (Job 7:16). He later said, "Are not my few days almost over? Turn away from me so I can have a moment's joy" (10:20).

Job knew the loneliness of suffering. Suffering often results in loneliness, doesn't it? When we hurt in body and in heart, we're prone to lose our perspective on life. Little things become big, and big things become much smaller.

We focus on ourselves, not on others; we look only at the painful present and not to the hopeful future. When we hurt, we're especially conscious of our own minds and bodies. We start questioning our faith and worrying. We become afraid. So often suffering results in loneliness.

A Description of Job's Suffering

Let's look at several aspects of Job's experience. Perhaps we can discover in the Word of God the encouragement we need when our suffering makes us feel lonely.

An Animal in a Net

Job 19 gives Job's interpretation of his situation. It's a very interesting chapter, filled with vivid pictures of what he was going through. In verse 6 Job says, "Know now that God hath overthrown me, and hath compassed me with his net" (KJV). This is the first picture he gave as he described his suffering: He saw himself as an animal caught in a net. "God has wronged me and drawn his net around me."

In the previous chapter, Job's friend Bildad talked about Job's situation, and he warned Job, "His feet thrust him into a net and he wanders into its mesh. A trap seizes him by the heel; a snare holds him fast" (18:8–9). Bildad said, in effect, "You're going to trap yourself, Job." But Job said, "No, God is the One who has trapped me in the net."

When you suffer, you feel as if you are trapped. You feel confined. All of a sudden you have lost your liberty. There you are in a cast or wearing a brace. There you are in a hospital bed being told what to do and what not to do. The doctor says you can't work and you can't have too many visitors. When you're suffering, you feel trapped—like an animal in a net.

A Criminal in Court

A second picture of Job's suffering is found in Job 19:7: "Though I cry, 'I've been wronged!' I get no response; though I call for help, there is no justice." One translation says, "Note this: I cry out because of violence" (MLB). Job pictured himself as a criminal in court, standing before God, the all-knowing judge. Job was protesting his situation and saying, "This is wrong! Why should this happen to me? I cry aloud, but there is no justice." Job felt guilty, and he thought that God was being unfair. He cried out, but God didn't even answer. That's a part of the loneliness of suffering. We cry out to God, and sometimes God doesn't answer right away. The silence of God makes our loneliness hurt that much more. Our faith is on trial. We stand in court, but there is nobody there to defend us.

Sometimes suffering brings back old guilt, the memory of past sins, the regrets of past errors and mistakes. We have a lot of time on our hands while we lie in a hospital bed, and it becomes more and more difficult to wait for God to answer.

A Traveler at a Roadblock

In Job 19:8 we see a third picture: "He [God] has blocked my way so I cannot pass; he has shrouded my paths in darkness." Job felt like a traveler at a roadblock. He was saying, "Here I was making such good progress, going forward in life. I was raising my children and I was enjoying my life. I was serving God." And he was. We must never get the idea that Job had been living a wicked life. Job had been living a life of service to glorify God. "Now," he said, "I'm like a traveler who can't go any farther. There's a roadblock in front of me. If I turn to the right, there's a hedge. If I turn to the left, there's a ditch. I can't go backward. I can't go forward."

Have you ever felt that way when you've been suffering? All your plans for future employment and enjoyment are changed and you have to sit still. There were so many things you were going to do, and then you had a heart attack. There were so many plans you were going to fulfill for yourself and your family, and then there was an auto accident. You became a traveler at a roadblock, unable to make progress. It's no wonder Job was frustrated. He was like an animal in a net, a criminal in a courtroom, a traveler at a roadblock.

A Dethroned King

In Job 19:9 we read: "He has stripped me of my honor and removed the crown from my head." Job saw himself as a king who had been dethroned. He had lost his glory.

He certainly had lost his physical glory. Job was sitting on the ash heap, covered with sores. He was ugly. When people looked at him, they shook their heads, closed their eyes, and turned away.

He had lost his financial glory. He was bankrupt. He had lost every bit of his financial resources. People were laughing at him behind his back. They were poking fun at him now that he was poor.

There was a time when Job was "on the throne." He told people what to do. He was respected and obeyed. But now he was on an ash heap, a broken man with a broken body, a man with no future. He was like a king dethroned.

Many times in my pastoral ministry I visited executives in hospitals—men who were accustomed to signing checks for thousands of dollars and giving orders to scores of people. Yet there they were in that hospital bed, with an anonymous nurse's aide telling them what to do. They were like dethroned kings at the mercy of other people, taking orders instead of giving them.

A Building Being Destroyed

Job 19:10 says, "He tears me down on every side till I am gone." It's the picture of the destruction of a building. In Scripture, the believer's body is often compared to a temple or a building. When you're suffering, you feel as if that building is being torn down, that God and His "demolition crew" have attacked you. There is pain, and sometimes the building doesn't function as it should. When suffering comes, it is so hard just to function normally the way we want to function. Job saw himself as a building being destroyed.

An Uprooted Tree

Job also saw himself as an uprooted tree: "He uproots my hope like a tree" (Job 19:10). Job said, "Here I was with my roots down deep, and I was growing and bearing fruit. There were people who found shade under my branches. Now I am not just cut down—I'm uprooted!" Job was a beautiful tree, and then along came the storm that uprooted him. It looked as though Job had no future. His hopes were gone.

If you pull up a tree by its roots, the tree will die. When you lose the roots in your life, there is not much future left. Your hope is gone.

An Enemy Besieged by God

Finally, Job saw himself as an enemy besieged by God's army: "His anger burns against me; he counts me among his enemies. His troops advance in force; they build a siege ramp against me and encamp around my tent" (Job 19:11–12). For years, God had been Job's friend, but now Job felt like

God was an enemy besieging him. Job experienced fear and danger because it seemed like God was against him. He could say with Jacob, "Everything is against me" (Gen. 42:36).

The Results of Job's Suffering

We can well understand why Job would feel lonely. Having described his suffering, Job then showed the results of this suffering (Job 19:13–21). "He has alienated my brothers from me; my acquaintances are completely estranged from me" (v. 13). That's a clear description of loneliness. "My kinsmen have gone away; my friends have forgotten me" (v. 14). Has that ever happened to you? "My guests and my maidservants count me a stranger; they look upon me as an alien. I summon my servant, but he does not answer, though I beg him with my own mouth" (vv. 15–16). You would think that a servant, who is being paid by the master, would respond; but even Job's personal servant would have nothing to do with him.

"My breath is offensive to my wife; I am loathsome to my own brothers" (v. 17). Job complains because his wife won't come near him and his relatives won't have anything to do with him. "Even the little boys scorn me" (v. 18). Usually young children are sympathetic toward older people who are hurting, but not in Job's neighborhood. "When I appear, they ridicule me. All my intimate friends detest me; those I love have turned against me" (v. 19).

No wonder he cried out in verse 21, "Have pity on me, my friends, have pity, for the hand of God has struck me." He felt alienated from everyone. This is the cry of loneliness! Job was once great in stature, in wealth, in power and authority, and in godliness, but now he was rejected and forgotten, even by his closest friends.

33

This is the loneliness that comes when we are suffering. It doesn't have to be physical affliction; it can be emotional affliction. It can be a broken heart as well as a broken body. Job was talking about the loneliness of suffering.

The Cure for Job's Suffering

I don't want to give only the diagnosis of the case, because when you're suffering and feeling lonely, when people have forgotten you, what is the answer? The answer is found in Job 19:25–26. The answer is Jesus Christ. "I know that my Redeemer lives, and that in the end he will stand upon the earth. And after my skin has been destroyed, yet in my flesh I will see God."

What was Job testifying about? He was saying, "I have a living Redeemer!" Job didn't know as much about Jesus Christ as we do; therefore, our faith ought to be greater than his. Job said, "I have a living Redeemer who one day is going to stand on this earth and make everything right. It's not important that I have everything my way today. What is important is that one day God will have everything His way when the Redeemer comes."

When you have a living Savior, then you have a living hope. "In my flesh I will see God" (v. 26). Job was describing his resurrection. The doctrine of the resurrection is found in the Old Testament, but not as clearly as it is in the New Testament. Job was looking forward to that time when all of his suffering would be over, all of his trials would end, and instead of suffering, he would experience glory.

When you realize that Jesus Christ is your Savior, that Jesus Christ is the Redeemer, that one day Jesus Christ will return and make everything the way it's supposed to be, you have hope. Even though your friends may forsake you, your family may neglect you, and the children pay no attention to you, Jesus is always there.

Christ Sets Us Free

Let's go back to the pictures that Job gave of his suffering and see what a difference Jesus can make. Job felt like an animal confined in a net, but with Jesus Christ as your Savior, you have freedom. "So if the Son sets you free, you will be free indeed" (John 8:36).

In Philippians 4:11 Paul said, "I have learned to be content whatever the circumstances." Paul was in prison, and like Job, he was like an animal in a net. Yet Paul said, "I am free! They might confine my body, but they can't confine my soul. I'm free in the Lord Jesus Christ!"

Christ Represents Us

Job felt like a criminal standing in court with no one to defend him. But Romans 8:38–39 tells us that *nothing* can separate us from the love of Christ. Who can condemn us when Christ has died for us and today represents us in heaven before the throne of God (v. 34)? "Therefore, there is now no condemnation for those who are in Christ Jesus" (v. 1). Jesus intercedes for us in heaven (v. 34) and ministers as our advocate (1 John 2:1–2). We are not on trial, for God's throne is a throne of grace and not a throne of judgment (Heb. 4:14–16).

Christ Guides Us

Job felt like a traveler facing a roadblock; he didn't know which way to go. But we have a Savior, the Good Shepherd, who guides us. "The steps of a good man are ordered by the LORD" (Ps. 37:23 KJV)—and so are the steps of a good man!

You may be in a situation now where God is making you lie down (Ps. 23:2), but you can be sure He knows what He's doing. The Savior guides us as long as we're willing to follow.

We Reign through Christ

Job felt like a king who had been dethroned, but as Christians we are not dethroned. Romans 5:17 tells us that we "reign in life through the one man, Jesus Christ." Jesus has made us to be "a kingdom and priests" (Rev. 1:6). When we turn the throne of our lives over to Jesus, He invites us to join Him on the throne so that together we "reign in life." He doesn't reign instead of us or in spite of us, but with us and through us as we love and obey Him.

We Are Built Up Eternally in Christ

Job said that he felt like a building being torn down piece by piece. As we get older, we may start to feel the same way. But 2 Corinthians 4:16 assures us that "though our outward man perish, yet the inward man is renewed day by day" (KJV). It's easy to focus on the outward person, the physical body that's aging and falling apart, but the Christian focuses on the inward person, the sanctifying work of the Spirit that makes us more like Christ. After all, that's our destiny—to be like Jesus (1 John 3:1–3).

We Are Rooted in Christ

Job had lost his hope because he felt like a tree that was being uprooted. If you chop down a tree, it can sprout again; but when you root it up, that's the end. As Christians, we are rooted eternally in Jesus Christ. We have a living hope because we belong to the living Savior, the Lord Jesus Christ. This hope is part of our birthright because "he has given us new birth into a living hope" (1 Peter 1:3). We can be like trees planted by the living waters, bearing fruit to the glory of God (Ps. 1:3).

We Are Reconciled through Christ

Job felt like God was his enemy; but God is not our enemy. He is our faithful friend and our loving Father. We are "reconciled to him [God] through the death of his Son" (Rom. 5:10). Once we were enemies of God because of the way we thought and the way we acted, but Jesus ended the war by dying on the cross and paying for our sins. Not only are we reconciled to God, but we have the very life of God in our hearts. We are His children!

What I'm saying is this: Don't go by your feelings or you will make the same mistakes that Job made. Your feelings will make you think you're trapped in a net, or standing condemned in a court. Feelings are deceptive. You feel as if you're standing at a roadblock, unable to make any progress. Your throne is gone. Your body is a building that is being destroyed or a tree that is being uprooted. God seems like an enemy besieging you. When Jesus Christ is your Savior, when He moves in and controls your life, He makes the difference between defeat and victory. If you have trusted Christ, He is standing with you, praying for you, strengthening you, and enabling you to do what He wants you to do. This we accept by faith, and we don't succumb to our deceptive feelings. We live by faith in God's Word and rest completely in the promises of God and our exalted position in Christ.

Are you feeling lonely because of suffering? My word to you is simply this: If you've trusted Jesus Christ as your Savior, He is right there with you and you are not alone. If you know Him as your Lord, you can be encouraged today. "I consider that our present sufferings are not worth comparing with the glory that will be revealed in us" (Rom. 8:18).

Job said, "I know that my Redeemer lives." When you have a living Christ, you have a living hope, and there's no reason to give up. "He who began a good work in you will carry it on to completion until the day of Christ Jesus" (Phil. 1:6).

4

Moses
THE LONELINESS OF SERVICE

"A leader does not deserve the name," wrote Henry A. Kissinger, "unless he is willing occasionally to stand alone."

What is there about leadership that creates loneliness? First of all, the position itself. Leadership means being over people and leading them. When Peter wrote to the elders in 1 Peter 5, he reminded them that they were *over* the people ("overseers") and also *among* the people (sheep in the flock). That's a very difficult position because it creates a certain amount of tension. Your pastor is one of the sheep, and yet he is the shepherd leading the sheep. The tension of leadership can create loneliness.

I think, too, that those who are in places of leadership face the loneliness of making decisions. When he was president of the United States, Harry S. Truman said, "To be President of the United States is to be lonely, very lonely, at times of great decisions." Having to make decisions creates loneliness because of the consequences that are involved. You make a decision, you sign a paper, you share a vision, and many people are affected by the consequences.

Leaders are lonely because of the great demands made on their time and energy. Woodrow Wilson, when he was president of the United States, said this: "It's an awful thing to be President of the United States. It means giving up nearly everything that one holds dear. The presidency becomes a barrier between a man and his wife, between a man and his children." There are sacrifices to make if you are a faithful and conscientious leader.

The loneliness of leadership can show up especially in Christian ministry. When you're involved in Christian service, the demands on your schedule can rob you of precious time with your family. Service means sacrifice, and it's not always easy to balance the schedule.

I think one of the most lonely things about service is this: Those who are in leadership positions have to see further and deeper than other people. God gives leaders the vision of what can be done and the desire to see things happen to His glory. Sometimes the followers don't have that same vision and desire, and this creates problems for the leaders. Time after time Moses, Joshua, the prophets, and even our Lord Jesus Christ were misunderstood and resisted because their followers didn't catch their vision.

People who are in places of leadership are the targets of criticism, most of which is untrue, unkind, and unnecessary. Leaders become scapegoats. It may be a great privilege to be a leader, but with that privilege comes great responsibility and accountability. It's wonderful to be called by God to serve, whether you are a Sunday school teacher, chairman of a committee, chairman of a church board, pastor, missionary, or Christian executive. But no matter where you serve, you will discover the loneliness of leadership.

Moses discovered this truth while leading the Jewish people in the wilderness. His experience is recorded in Numbers 11:4–6:

The rabble with them began to crave other food, and again the Israelites started wailing and said, "If only we had meat to eat! We remember the fish we ate in Egypt at no cost—also the cucumbers, melons, leeks, onions and garlic. But now we have lost our appetite; we never see anything but this manna!"

For a year the Israelites had been eating the manna that came down from heaven, and it had nourished them adequately. God graciously sent it to them each morning except the Sabbath, but now they were tired of the manna and wanted something different. Their hearts were still in Egypt—and so were their appetites.

Moses heard the people of every family wailing, each at the entrance to his tent. The LORD became exceedingly angry, and Moses was troubled. He asked the LORD, "Why have you brought this trouble on your servant? What have I done to displease you that you put the burden of all these people on me? Did I conceive all these people? Did I give them birth? Why do you tell me to carry them in my arms, as a nurse carries an infant, to the land you promised on oath to their forefathers? Where can I get meat for all these people? . . . I cannot carry all these people by myself; the burden is too heavy for me. If this is how you are going to treat me, put me to death right now—if I have found favor in your eyes—and do not let me face my own ruin."

Numbers 11:10–15

Before you criticize Moses for expressing himself this way, you had better walk in his shoes for a while! He had the care of all the children of Israel there in the wilderness. They were a brand-new nation and were just starting to learn what it means to walk with God by faith and to follow His appointed leader. Israel was a nation of former slaves, just liberated from Egypt, and Moses was trying to mold them into a great nation. They had much to learn, and they still

41

remembered "the good old days" in Egypt. Unfortunately, they quickly forgot the bondage and burdens of those years of slavery. It took Moses one night to get the Jews out of Egypt, but it took forty years to get Egypt out of the Jews.

Leadership is not easy; it is very difficult and very costly. Serving others isn't easy; it is demanding. When you're discouraged and lonely in your service for Christ and you feel like giving up, just remind yourself of some of the lessons that Moses learned when he felt like giving up.

People Are Always People

Lesson number one: Remind yourself that people are always people. People are prone to complain simply because complaining is human. So often I've had the privilege of sharing in the installation service for a new pastor at a church. Often it's a young pastor, recently graduated from school and about to enter ministry. At some point in my private conversation I try to say to this young man, "Now, just remember, these are people you're pastoring. They aren't perfect. They never will be perfect until they see the Lord Jesus Christ."

People are always people. If you want to, you can avoid the problems of people by avoiding people. Don't be a leader. Don't be in a place of service. Just go off in a corner someplace and live with yourself. But if you are going to be a leader, you must remember that people are always people. They are prone to complain. Instead of remembering the blessings and appreciating your ministry, they are going to think about all the things they don't have. It's always better someplace else!

When I read Numbers 11:5, I'm shocked: "We remember the fish we ate in Egypt at no cost." Can you imagine the Jews saying that? It cost them a great deal to eat the fish, the leeks, the onions, and the garlic. It cost them their freedom! They were slaves in Egypt! They forgot that fact, and they forgot what Moses had done for them and how God had provided for them and guided them. People are always people. They are prone to complain.

Because people are always people, they will always think the past was better. I don't know how many times I've heard that in my ministry. "When Pastor So-and-So was pastor of this church, those were the good old days!" I once asked an elderly church member what people were talking about in the good old days, and he said, "Well, they were talking about the good old days." People forget the blessings of the present and get caught up in the so-called "good old days" of the past. People are rarely excited about the prospects of the future. They want to duplicate the great days of the past, because to them, the past is always better.

Because people are always people, they tend to exaggerate their problems. Everything that comes along is the worst thing that ever happened. They also have a tendency to lose their spiritual momentum. When Israel was delivered from Egypt, they were at a spiritual peak. They were delivered in great power and went through the Red Sea in great victory. They sang a song of praise to the Lord. But before long, they began to complain. God met their need, but they started complaining all over again, and God had to discipline them.

People have a tendency to lose their spiritual momentum. The monotony of the land and the journey was bothering Israel. The sameness of the diet aggravated them. Sad to say, they were getting accustomed to their blessings.

I notice something else: People are easily influenced by others. The mixed multitude ("rabble") was that unbelieving crowd that left Egypt with the Israelites. They were not Jewish people but Egyptians who joined the exodus and left Egypt with the Jewish nation. The mixed multitude in the church—this unconverted crowd—likes to complain. In every church and Christian assembly there are people who like to complain, and their complaining spreads and infects others.

When you are discouraged, lonely, and tempted to give up, remember this first lesson: People are always people. Have high ideals for God's people, but be realistic.

Everything Looks Worse Than It Is

A second lesson for leaders is this: The situation always looks worse than it really is. The Israelites were crying out for something to eat, and Moses was saying to God, "Where can I get flesh to feed all of these people?" I notice in Numbers 11:11–14 that Moses repeated the phrase, "All these people." The situation always looks worse than it really is, especially when you walk by sight and not by faith.

When Israel was delivered from Egypt, they stood at the Red Sea with the Egyptian army behind them, the desert around them, and the sea before them. Could the situation have been more difficult? Yet God opened the way and saw them through. Later, they cried out for water, and God gave them water. They had to have food, so God gave them manna. One day the Amalekites showed up and declared war on them, and God gave Israel the victory. How quick we are to forget what God has done for us! Charles Spurgeon used to say that we are prone to write our blessings in the sand and engrave our complaints in marble. We forget what God has done.

If you are in a situation right now that looks very difficult, the devil wants it to look far worse than it really is. Unbelief says, "Oh, this is terrible!" When the twelve Jewish spies went into the land of Canaan to survey the situation, they saw the giants and the high walls, but they didn't see God. They came back and said, "We are like grasshoppers next to those great giants!" (see Num. 13:33). They forgot how big their God really was. God is great! The situation always looks worse than it really is if you take your eyes off the Lord and start looking at yourself and your problems.

Leaders Often Magnify Their Own Importance

There is a third lesson to be learned from Moses' situation: It's very easy for leaders to magnify their own importance. Moses started to pout. "Why have you brought this trouble on your servant? What have I done to displease you that you put the burden of all these people on me?" (see Num. 11:11).

I want to give Moses credit for expressing himself honestly. Moses didn't get up and make some pious speech. He went off and prayed and told God how he felt. That's a good way to respond when it seems like everybody is against you and the problems are too great to be solved. When you read the Book of Psalms, you discover the psalmist didn't use artificial, pious prayers. He told God exactly how he felt. "My God, my God, why have you forsaken me? Why are you so far from saving me?" (Ps. 22:1). But Moses was magnifying his own importance. *He* had to get food for all the people. Nobody could do it but Moses!

We who are in the Lord's service aren't responsible for the spiritual maturity or immaturity of our people if we have been faithful in feeding them God's Word. You couldn't have found a more faithful leader than Moses. In fact, the writer of the Book of Hebrews says he was "faithful in all God's house" (Heb. 3:2, 5). Moses was faithful to do what God gave him to do, yet the people remained immature.

45

Moses should not have taken the blame or magnified his own importance.

Don't have a messianic complex. Don't think you have to solve every problem, perform every miracle, or meet every need. God is the One who is in control. It is easy to magnify our own importance. Notice how many personal pronouns are in Moses' prayer. Moses was looking at himself instead of looking by faith to the Lord.

Leadership Is a Privilege

We need to learn a fourth lesson concerning the loneliness of service: Leadership is a privilege, and the burdens help to balance the blessings.

Don't misunderstand me; there are burdens to leadership. I've pastored three churches and ministered in two different parachurch organizations. I've served on mission boards and ministered in many parts of the world. I realize from experience that leaders have their share of burdens. That's a part of life. But to every dedicated leader, God says, "I'll help you carry the burden. You aren't doing it alone."

Yes, there are burdens to leadership; but Moses forgot about the privileges. "You have laid the burden of all these people on me. Have I conceived all these people? Should I carry them the way a father carries a little child?" (see Num. 11:11–12). In their newfound freedom, the Jews were like little children who didn't know how to behave, and Moses' task wasn't an easy one. But God never expected him to carry the burdens himself.

Moses lost the glow of leadership. Moses lost the excitement of the privilege of being God's chosen leader to serve Him personally. Perhaps your Sunday school class is breaking your heart just now, but it's a privilege to be teaching the Word of God. Maybe people on your mission field are not responding the way they should, but it's a privilege to be sharing the Gospel with them. Your church may not be growing as it should, but what a privilege to be one of God's servants. Remember, the angels in heaven would gladly change places with us. They would wait on the brink of glory and rush to have the privilege of preaching and teaching the Word of God. But God doesn't use the angels to do the work of gospel ministry. He uses weak vessels of clay like Moses—and like you and me.

God Will Solve the Problems

Leadership is a privilege, not a burden. There are burdens to leadership, but those burdens turn out to be blessings when we let God have control. And that leads to our final lesson: God can and will solve all the problems. Just do what Moses did: Go to God in prayer. Tell Him how you feel. Tell Him what's wrong. Tell Him what you think needs to be done. And then listen to Him and obey whatever He says.

In the rest of Numbers 11, God told Moses what to do. Moses was to share the blessing and the burden of his ministry with seventy elders of the people. Moses obeyed, the Spirit came down in power, the workload was shared, and the need was met.

Leaders must talk to God. Apart from prayer, it's impossible to have the wisdom and power we need to serve God.

Leaders must trust God, for "without faith it is impossible to please God" (Heb. 11:6). Faith is the secret of answered prayer and moving mountains. A leader without faith is like a jet plane without engines.

Leaders must obey God, because true faith leads to obedience. Faith means obeying God in spite of how we feel, what we see, or what the consequences may be. A true leader finds out what God wants done and then does it by faith, to the glory of the Lord.

Moses said "I am not" (v. 14), but God's name is I AM (Exod. 3:14). Whenever you say "I am not," just remember that God says "I AM." The Lord "is able to do immeasurably more than all we ask or imagine" (Eph. 3:20), because His calling is also His enabling. If God has called you, He will equip you. If God has called you, He will enlighten you. If God has called you, He will enable you. If God has called you, He will encourage you. He will see you through. Therefore, don't pray as Moses did and ask God to take away your ministry or (even worse) your life (see Num. 11:15). Instead say, "Lord, You do the work, You get the glory. Give me what I need. Give me the divine enablement to glorify Your name." God will see you through.

Yes, there is loneliness in leadership, but there is also blessing in serving Jesus as we seek to glorify Him and patiently love and serve His people.

5

Elijah
THE LONELINESS OF SELF-PITY

First Kings 19 introduces us to a remarkable experience in the life of a great servant of God, the prophet Elijah. He had just defeated the priests of Baal on Mount Carmel; but after winning the battle, he lost the victory. He ended up running away from the place of duty, trudging alone through the desert, wallowing in self-pity, a powerful preacher who was lonely and discouraged.

In the United States, more than four million people per year receive special care because of depression. Often, depression is a result of loneliness, the kind of loneliness that feeds on self-pity. We don't like to talk about self-pity. We'd rather defend our own egos and maintain our self-esteem. But self-pity can be one of the most poisonous things in our system. When we start nurturing self-pity, we open ourselves up to all kinds of problems.

First Kings 18 records Elijah's victory over Baal. God answered prayer and sent fire from heaven to prove that He alone is the true God. The people had fallen on their faces crying, "The LORD—he is God! The LORD—he is God!" (v. 39), and the prophets of Baal were slain by the servants of God. Then God sent the much-needed rain and ended over three years of drought. It was indeed a high and holy day in Israel.

You would think that after all this blessing Elijah would have been walking on the mountain peaks of victory, but just the opposite took place. He was miserable, ran away, and ended up in a cave watching a storm.

> Now Ahab told Jezebel everything Elijah had done and how he had killed all the prophets with the sword. So Jezebel sent a messenger to Elijah to say, "May the gods deal with me, be it ever so severely, if by this time tomorrow I do not make your life like that of one of them." Elijah was afraid and ran for his life. When he came to Beersheba in Judah, he left his servant there, while he himself went a day's journey into the desert. He came to a broom tree, sat down under it and prayed that he might die. "I have had enough, LORD," he said. "Take my life; I am no better than my ancestors." Then he lay down under the tree and fell asleep. All at once an angel touched him and said, "Get up and eat." He looked around, and there by his head was a cake of bread baked over hot coals, and a jar of water. He ate and drank and then lay down again. The angel of the LORD came back a second time and touched him and said, "Get up and eat, for the journey is too much for you." So he got up and ate and drank. Strengthened by that food, he traveled forty days and forty nights until he reached Horeb, the mountain of God. There he went into a cave and spent the night.
>
> 1 Kings 19:1–9

Let's consider some of the truths that are found in this record of Elijah's experience, truths that can help us in our own lives today.

The Cost of Self-Pity

Elijah was wallowing in self-pity. "I want to die!" he said. If he had really meant that, Jezebel would have taken care of it for him. Had Elijah really wanted to die, all he had to do was to say to Jezebel, "Here I am; take my life." The ultimate self-pity is wanting your life to end, and tragically, thousands take that route and commit suicide. But why do we permit self-pity to take control of our lives?

Loss of Perspective

When we encourage self-pity, we lose our perspective. Everything becomes "out of joint." The little things become big, and the big things don't seem too important anymore. If would-be suicides would talk their problems over with an understanding friend they would regain their perspective and never destroy themselves. We should never make important decisions while we're discouraged and indulging in self-pity, because we'll make the wrong decision.

Elijah had just slain the false prophets of Baal, yet one woman frightened him. He had called down fire from heaven, yet one woman caused him to flee his post. Yes, Jezebel was the queen and was an evil woman, but Elijah's self-pity had caused him to lose his perspective. When we lose our perspective, we exaggerate the way we feel and we tend to get the wrong picture of the circumstances around us. We exaggerate what other people are doing to us and saying about us. Self-pity is an expensive luxury and a terrible master.

51

Loss of Patience

Not only do we lose our perspective, but we also lose our patience. We get impulsive and refuse to wait on the Lord and, like Elijah, we run away from our place of ministry and blessing. "Elijah was afraid and ran for his life" (1 Kings 19:3). He didn't wait on the Lord and seek God's direction. You can't help but notice in the record of Elijah's life that whenever he succeeded, it was because he obeyed what God told him to do. "The word of the LORD came unto him, saying" is an oft-repeated phrase (17:2, 8; 18:1). But this time we find Elijah impulsively, impatiently running ahead of God.

Be careful when you start getting nervous and fidgety, because you are liable to do something stupid. The Bible says, "He that believeth shall not make haste" (Isa. 28:16 KJV). Patience is important in the Christian life, but indulging in self-pity will transform impatience into reckless disobedience. "Do not fret—it leads only to evil" (Ps. 37:8).

Loss of Personal Touch

Self-pity is expensive. It not only causes us to lose our perspective and our patience, but it also causes us to lose our personal touch. We get isolated and insulated and believe that we're the only faithful servant left. Elijah should have been ministering to the people, but instead he ran off by himself, even leaving his servant behind. He was solitary, and that solitude gradually turned into loneliness.

We need other people and they need us. We can't make it in the Christian life all by ourselves. The journey is too great for us. We must have the Lord walking with us and the Lord's people encouraging us. I thank God for His people. They've been an encouragement and help to me. At this point Elijah needed their help more than ever before. "But he was a great prophet," someone argues. "He could pray and marvelous things would happen." That's true, but he was also a man of like nature as we are (James 5:17), and he needed that personal touch. He couldn't succeed alone.

Loss of Purpose

In addition to losing our personal touch, self-pity can make us lose our sense of purpose. The prophet prayed that God would take his life, but God didn't call Elijah so He could kill him. God called Elijah to use him to restore the people of Israel to the worship of the true God. Elijah forgot that he was a man under orders and that God called him to fulfill a divine purpose.

In my own ministry, I've often heard from pastors and other Christian workers who are having a difficult time serving the Lord. They say, "You know, I'd just as soon throw it all overboard and quit! It's just not worth it!" Then they start praying as Elijah prayed, "Oh, Lord, let me die!" But this unbelief is nothing new. One dark day, even Moses prayed, "If this is how you are going to treat me, put me to death right now" (Num. 11:15).

Before you quit and run away, seriously consider the high cost of self-pity. If we feed our ego by wallowing in self-pity, God may not stop us, but what a terrible price we pay. Suppose God had answered Elijah's prayer and taken his life? Would the work have come to a halt? No, because God had Elisha prepared to take his place. If Elijah had died, the work of God would have gone on, because nobody is indispensible in God's kingdom. If Elijah's prayer had been answered, he would have missed a glorious chariot ride to heaven!

If you find yourself wallowing in self-pity, enjoying it, licking your wounds, feeling sorry for yourself, and even wanting to die, just remember the tremendous price you are paying. Is it worth it?

The Causes of Self-Pity

Physical

Self-pity often has physical causes. James 5:17 tells us that Elijah was a man of like nature as we are and suffered the same temptations and problems that we suffer. Elijah was weary and hungry, so God gave him something to eat and drink, and he took a nap. An angel baked fresh bread for him, and from the food, water, and rest, Elijah got enough strength to continue his journey for forty days and nights. The prophet was empowered by the Spirit in a wonderful way, but he wasn't taking proper care of his body and he suffered the consequences. Too many busy Christian workers are on the verge of burnout and don't realize it. They forget the familiar motto: Beware the barrenness of a busy life.

Sometimes we who are in Christian service don't take good care of our bodies. We wonder why we're discouraged and feeling sorry for ourselves. It may be that your body chemistry has been upset, or perhaps your body is screaming at you, "Slow down! Get some sleep!" When we're tired and haven't eaten properly, the body doesn't function as it should, and we reap the depressing consequences.

Emotional

But there was also an emotional cause for Elijah's self-pity. He had just been through a tremendous crisis on Mount Carmel and the strain of an all-day meeting. Pastors should be careful on Mondays. Monday follows Sunday, the most

54

difficult day in a minister's life. I know from experience how many Monday mornings everything seems dark and discouraging. There are emotional causes for self-pity, especially when we've gone through crises and heavy demands are made on us. How easy it is to go from the mountaintop of glory to the valley of despair!

Spiritual

There are also spiritual causes of self-pity. I think this was the real problem for Elijah, although the other things we've mentioned certainly factor in. To begin with, Elijah was guilty of unbelief. In 1 Kings 19:3 we read, "When he saw that, he arose" (KJV). He was walking by sight and not by faith. He "went for his life" (v. 3). He was walking selfishly because he wasn't thinking about God's will or God's work. "The man who loves his life will lose it," said Jesus, "while the man who hates his life in this world will keep it for eternal life" (John 12:25).

Elijah was at low ebb spiritually because he felt he had failed. He said, "I am no better than my ancestors" (1 Kings 19:4). When did God ever say that His servants should be better than those who came before them? Elijah's job wasn't to compete with the great men of the past but to complete the work God had given him to do. He felt that he had failed and that the people of Israel had failed. Don't compare yourself with any other servant of God, because we're all different and have different gifts and opportunities. God won't use us on the basis of what Moses or David or Paul did, but on the basis of what we are called to do.

When he met God at the cave, Elijah said, "I am the only one left" (19:10), but God replied that there were seven thousand people in the land who had not bowed the knee to Baal (v. 18). "I'm the only faithful believer left!" is a confession that reeks of pride, unbelief, and ignorance. David wrote, "Help, LORD, for the godly are no more" (Ps. 12:1), and the prophet Micah wrote, "The godly have been swept from the land; not one upright man remains" (Micah 7:2). An anonymous psalmist confessed, "And in my dismay I said, 'All men are liars'" (Ps. 116:11). The Lord knows who His people are, where they are, how many there are, and how faithful they are. For us to start fretting about this matter means developing either deep discouragement or inflated pride, both of which are sins.

Elijah felt that God had failed. It's as though he said, "God, why didn't You bring a great revival to the nation? Why aren't they all worshiping You?" He was discouraged by a sense of failure. But he didn't stay on the job long enough to follow up on the great work God had done at Mount Carmel. He needed to heed the words of Andrew Bonar who said, "We must be as watchful after the victory as before the battle." Elijah had won the battle but lost the victory.

When we feel as if we've failed, we must never give up. We must never quit. Only God knows whether or not we've failed or succeeded, and we must do our best and leave the rest with Him. God rarely allows His servants to see all the good they are doing. One day in heaven we will find out what God has accomplished through us. Self-esteem and statistics are not important. All that matters is whether God has been glorified.

There are physical causes of self-pity. Maybe you need a good night's rest, a good meal, some exercise, some ventilation. There are emotional causes. Perhaps you've been through a demanding and difficult time and need to get away and relax. But fundamentally there are spiritual causes: unbelief, trying to measure our own ministry, feeding our own ego, and forgetting about God's glory.

The Cure for Self-Pity

If anybody had a right to feel sorry for herself, it was Helen Keller, who was blind and deaf from the age of nineteen months. Yet, she called self-pity our worst enemy. The patient ministry of her teacher, Anne Sullivan, brought her out of the dark and into a fruitful life. There are some definite steps we can take to overcome self-pity and begin to live once again for the Lord and for others.

Look to the Lord

In 1 Kings 19:8–18, we read that God met Elijah at Mount Horeb. How wonderful it is that God condescends to meet us when we are at our lowest and doubting Him the most! As Elijah stood on the mountain, the wind blew, an earthquake shook the mountain, and a fire came from the Lord—but the Lord was not in the wind, the earthquake, or the fire. Then a still, small voice spoke to Elijah and told him what to do.

What is the cure for self-pity? First of all, look to the Lord. Just take yourself by the nape of the neck, shake yourself, and say, "I'm not going to look at myself. I'm not going to look at my failures or the failures of other people. I'm not going to look at the circumstances. I'm going to look to the Lord." Elijah had not failed, the people had not failed, and the circumstances were just what God ordained them to be. Your perspective changes when you see things from God's point of view.

I like that phrase—"a still, small voice" (v. 12 KJV) or "a gentle whisper" (NIV). God doesn't always accomplish His will in big noisy ways such as earthquakes, winds, and fires. On Mount Carmel, God sent a fire that consumed the sacrifice, because that was the sign the pagan priests expected; but when God came to Elijah, He spoke in a quiet voice.

God's Word accomplishes God's will, and God doesn't have to shout.

God has many tools for accomplishing His work. God can use the wind, the earthquake, and the fire, but ultimately God uses His Word—His still, small voice—to change people's minds and hearts. So, when you're discouraged and nurturing your self-pity, get your eyes off yourself and look to the Lord.

Talk to the Lord

Second, talk to the Lord and be honest with Him. Tell Him how you feel. Tell Him that you hurt. God sees our hearts and knows more about us than we know about ourselves, but He wants to hear us express ourselves. Elijah was wrong in some of the things he said, but he wasn't wrong in saying them. We're commanded to come to God with "confidence" (Heb. 4:16), which is the translation of the Greek word that means "freedom and openness of speech" (see Heb. 10:19; 1 John 2:28; 3:21; 4:17).

Prayer is one of the greatest privileges of the Christian life. The Father invites us to come at any time and share any need with Him. We have promises in His Word that encourage us in prayer. When we're discouraged, it's especially helpful to pray with other Christians, because there's power in united prayer.

Listen to the Lord

"Be still, and know that I am God" (Ps. 46:10 KJV). Listen to God's Word as He speaks to us through it. Read the Bible for yourself, or listen to it being read and expounded. God may send some word of encouragement and promise through one of His own people. Occasionally, I've felt like

Elijah and gone to hear somebody preach, and the message I heard was just what my heart needed. The Lord may even send you a special message in everyday conversation. We never know when the Lord may want to say something to us, so we must pay attention. Elijah learned that night that God had a plan and that he would be a part of the plan until the Lord took him to heaven.

Wait on the Lord

Look to the Lord, talk to the Lord, listen to the Lord, and wait on the Lord. Wait for His timing, because there are times and seasons to God's work and blessing (Gal. 6:9). Wait for His way to open and His plan to unfold. Most of us are activists and find it hard to wait on the Lord, but waiting is a time of growth, insight, and maturity. "But those who wait on the LORD shall renew their strength; they shall mount up with wings like eagles, they shall run and not be weary, they shall walk and not faint" (Isa. 40:31 NKJV).

Elijah illustrates the truths in that familiar verse. On Mount Carmel, he mounted up like the eagle, because he had just spent three years hiding himself and walking close to the Lord (1 Kings 17:3; 18:1). When the drought ended and the rains came, Elijah ran before Ahab's chariot and didn't get weary (18:41–46). But when he started walking in the wilderness, the journey was too much for him; he had to stop and allow the Lord to minister to him. Then he was able to walk forty days and nights in the strength the Lord provided (19:1–8). It pays to wait upon the Lord.

Let me warn you against cultivating self-pity. You'll lose your perspective and your patience. You will either pull into yourself and become isolated, or you will impulsively do some foolish thing that will embarrass the Lord and harm your life and ministry. You will lose that personal touch and get isolated and lonely, and you may forfeit the purpose God has for your life.

Instead, when you find yourself depressed, look to the Lord, talk to the Lord, listen to the Lord, and wait on the Lord. Dark days of discouragement and self-pity will eventually pass away and the sun will shine again. The longer we look inward, the darker life will become; so let's look upward and enjoy the healing light of the Lord. "Wait on the LORD; be of good courage, and he shall strengthen your heart; wait, I say, on the LORD" (Ps. 27:14 NKJV).

6

Mary and Martha
THE LONELINESS OF SORROW

Perhaps the most difficult kind of loneliness is the kind that comes from a sorrowing heart, the loneliness of bereavement. The Bible tells us that death is an enemy (see 1 Cor. 15:26). Yes, we know that God's people will go to heaven through faith in Jesus Christ, and we know that our loved ones in Christ go to be with the Lord when they die. This comforts our hearts, but we still hurt and need time to heal. Bereavement is something like an amputation: When a loved one dies, it feels like a part of you has been cut off. Even if we had the loved one with us for many years, that doesn't make the loss easier. It fact, it usually makes it harder.

It isn't wrong for Christians to grieve. It's wrong for Christians to grieve as unbelievers "who have no hope" (1 Thess. 4:13). In the Word of God, you find God's people weeping as they pass through the valley of the shadow of death. Abraham wept over Sarah when she died (Genesis 23); Joseph and his brothers wept when Jacob their father died (Genesis 50); and Jesus wept when he stood at the tomb of his beloved friend Lazarus (John 11).

Let's focus on John 11, the familiar story of the sickness, death, and resurrection of Lazarus. Lazarus was ill, and his two sisters sent a message to Jesus. "Lord, the one you love is sick" (v. 3). Our Lord tarried for two days, and during that time Lazarus died. Then Jesus went to Bethany. By the time He got there, Lazarus had been in the grave for four days. But Jesus raised Lazarus from the dead! Before He did that, however, He tenderly comforted Martha and Mary as they shared their grief with Him.

Martha was the more active of the two sisters. She went out immediately to meet Jesus when He arrived, but Mary remained in the house. Jesus asked for Mary, so she went out to see Him, and the neighbors who were there to comfort the sisters went out with her. Mary was weeping and the friends were weeping with her. When Jesus saw Mary and her friends weeping, He was deeply troubled and wept (v. 35).

A great deal of weeping is recorded in this chapter, but Jesus didn't criticize anyone for shedding tears. It isn't wrong for Christians to sorrow. It is wrong for Christians to sorrow as those who have no hope. God made us with tear ducts so we could weep, and that weeping helps us to heal inside. God's promise is, "Weeping may remain for a night, but rejoicing comes in the morning" (Ps. 30:5).

How can we find comfort and encouragement in times of loneliness and sorrow? We must claim the assurances that God gives us. John 11 contains a number of assurances that can help in times of loneliness and sorrow.

God Loves You

First of all, when they go through times of sorrow, believers can be sure they are the objects of God's love. I can understand why Mary and Martha might have questioned the love of Jesus. To begin with, their brother got sick; yet he was a beloved friend of our Lord (vv. 1–3). Some people claim that if you're walking in the will of God, you will never experience sickness and pain, but that wasn't true of Lazarus. We have no reason to believe that Lazarus was out of the will of God, and yet he became sick. The two sisters didn't question Jesus' love when they saw their brother sick and in pain, for they said in their message to Jesus, "Lord, the one you love is sick" (v. 3).

Love and Suffering

Suffering is not incompatible with love. Sometimes hurting people say, "If God loved me, He'd keep me from having accidents and from getting sick." But many times our sickness and accidents are our own fault and we can blame our own carelessness. If God intervened every time we were heading for a calamity, this world would be in a mess and nobody would ever build godly character or learn how to make wise decisions. Suffering is not incompatible with love; the cross of Jesus Christ is all the proof we need of that statement.

Love and Delay

Mary and Martha might have questioned God's love because of the Lord's delay. "Yet when he [Jesus] heard that Lazarus was sick, he stayed where he was two more days" (v. 6). The disciples might have argued, "If you really love Lazarus, you will rush to Bethany now and heal his sickness." But Jesus didn't hurry. He waited. Love and delay often go together. Jesus always knows the right time to come to heal our broken hearts.

Love and Disappointment

God's love might be questioned when we look at Lazarus's disease, our Lord's delay, and the sisters' disappointment.

Jesus had told them their brother's sickness would not end in death but would glorify God (v. 4); yet Lazarus did die. When Martha met Jesus, she said to Him, "Lord, if you had been here, my brother would not have died" (John 11:21). Mary said the same thing (v. 32). In verse 37, the friends who were visiting the two sisters said, "Could not he who opened the eyes of the blind man have kept this man from dying?"

So often when we're experiencing bereavement we say, "Oh, if we had only done this or that, our loved one might still be alive." But such talk only makes the sorrow worse. God loves us. Circumstances and feelings may cause us to question that, but God does love us. When we walk with the Lord by faith and obey Him, there are no ifs to fret over.

Love and God's Word

How do we know that God loves us? Because the Word of God tells us so. How do we know that Jesus loved this family? The Word of God says so. "Jesus loved Martha and her sister and Lazarus" (John 11:5). The Bible states very clearly that God loved these people. In spite of this love, the family experienced sickness, death, and sorrow. Never judge the love of God by your feelings or by your circumstances. Even the neighbors noticed the love Jesus had, because they said, "See how he loved him!" (v. 36).

The Bible tells us God loves us, and that settles the matter. We read in Romans 8:35 and 37–39:

> Who shall separate us from the love of Christ? Shall trouble or hardship or persecution or famine or nakedness or danger or sword? . . . No, in all these things we are more than conquerors through him who loved us. For I am convinced that neither death nor life, neither angels nor demons, neither the present nor the future, nor any powers, neither height nor depth, nor anything else in all creation, will be

able to separate us from the love of God that is in Christ Jesus, our Lord.

We know that God loves us because His Word tells us so. We know that God loves us because the Holy Spirit in our hearts tells us so. "God has poured out his love into our hearts by the Holy Spirit, whom He has given us" (Rom. 5:5). But the greatest proof of God's love to us is the cross of Jesus Christ. "God demonstrates his own love for us in this: While we were still sinners, Christ died for us" (v. 8).

No matter how much our hearts pain us, we can rest with assurance on the truth that God loves us.

Christ Is with You

Today, we who believe in Christ have an advantage that Mary and Martha didn't have: Jesus Christ is with all of His people all of the time and cannot be separated from them. When Jesus was here on earth, He was limited by His physical body. He had to leave where He was and travel to Bethany to comfort the two sisters. But today, our Lord is always with us. "Never will I leave you; never will I forsake you" is His promise (Heb. 13:5). The fact that He is constantly with us gives us several encouragements.

He Knows Your Sorrow

Jesus Christ knows our sorrows, what caused them, and what must be done to heal them. "Record my lament; list my tears on your scroll—are they not in your record?" (Ps. 56:8). The suggestion here is that God keeps a record of our tears and always knows the things that pain us.

God knows your sorrow. You may think God is too busy running the universe to take care of your broken heart, but

Psalm 147:3–4 says just the opposite: "He heals the bro-kenhearted and binds up their wounds. He determines the number of the stars and calls them each by name." God is not so busy numbering and naming the stars that He doesn't see your broken heart and know how to heal it. The God of the galaxies is the God who heals the brokenhearted.

He Shares Your Sorrow

Christ not only knows your sorrow, but He shares your sorrow. "Jesus wept" (John 11:35). The Lord Jesus is "a man of sorrows, and familiar with suffering" (Isa. 53:3). He groaned inwardly when He saw the tragedy that sin and death have brought into the world. Jesus knew He would raise Lazarus from the dead, but He was still indignant at the work of the last enemy, death (see 1 Cor. 15:26). Our glorified High Priest in heaven identifies with our feelings and sympathizes with our weaknesses. Grieving people often feel as though nobody knows how they feel, but you can be sure that Jesus knows. When He was here on earth, He tasted suffering, sorrow, and death, and He knows how they feel.

He Can Transform Your Sorrow

Jesus knows your sorrow, He shares your sorrow, and He can transform your sorrow. He said to Martha, "I am the resurrection and the life. He who believes in me will live, even though he dies; and whoever lives and believes in me will never die" (John 11:25–26). When you have Jesus Christ as your Savior, you don't have to worry about confronting death. He can transform and sanctify your sorrow because He has conquered death.

The Lord Jesus is "the resurrection and the life" (v. 25). For the believer, death is only sleep; the body goes to sleep and the soul goes to be with Jesus (1 Thess. 4:13–18). Jesus said in John 11:11, "Our friend Lazarus has fallen asleep." In death, the believer's body sleeps in the grave while the spirit goes home to be with the Lord. Knowing that Jesus is victorious over death, we can go through the valley with Him and not be afraid.

Believers who die in Christ are more alive in heaven than they ever were when they were with us on earth. Believers who are alive wnen Jesus returns will be transformed and become like Him, and they will go to be with Him forever. The blessed hope of our Lord's return transforms us and prepares us for that great event.

Assurance number one is that God loves you. Assurance number two is that Christ is with you. He is Immanuel, "God with us" (see Matt. 1:23). A third assurance is that God knows what He is doing and His will is best.

God's Will Is Best

God has His times and His purposes. The disciples couldn't understand why Jesus waited for two days, but Jesus explained, "Are there not twelve hours of daylight?" (John 11:9). In other words, "I'm on a divine timetable and I have My schedule. Don't rush Me." God has His times, and His timetable is never wrong. His delays are not denials but doorways to greater blessing.

God also has His purposes. One purpose God was accomplishing in the death of Lazarus was the strengthening of faith. Jesus said to IIis perplexed disciples, "For your sake I am glad I was not there, so that you may believe" (v. 15). The faith of the disciples was increased because they shared this difficult experience with Mary and Martha. Little by little, the disciples were learning what Jesus could do in the difficult circumstances of life. When the situation seemed hopeless, they could trust Him.

The faith of Martha and Mary was also strengthened, as was the faith of their friends who came to mourn with them. In fact, we are told that many of these friends believed in the Lord Jesus because He raised Lazarus from the dead (v. 45). Because Lazarus became ill and died, the Lord was able to bring many people to Himself.

I don't know what purpose God is fulfilling in your suffering, sorrow, and loneliness, but He knows what He's doing, and that's all that matters. We all go through difficult experiences and wonder why they happen. Mary and Martha didn't know God's purpose, for they both said, "Lord, if You had been here" (vv. 21, 32). Their friends echoed the sentiment (v. 37). In times of bereavement, bury the alternatives. Forget about the ifs. Just keep in mind that God's will is best. He has His times, and He will work out His purposes.

God Will Be Glorified If You Believe

A fourth assurance that can comfort you when you're experiencing the loneliness of sorrow is that God will be glorified if you believe. That's the promise that Jesus gave in John 11:4: "This sickness will not end in death. No, it is for God's glory so that God's Son may be glorified through it." Lazarus died, but that wasn't the end. Jesus raised him from the dead. It's not important that you and I escape sorrow, but it is important that God is glorified.

You may say, "But that's a difficult experience for people to go through just for the glory of God." But the glory of God is the most important thing in the universe! It was difficult for Jesus to die on the cross for the glory of God, but

He did it—and He did it for you. God will be glorified if you believe and let Him have His way.

Jesus said to the people, "Take away the stone" (v. 39); but Martha resisted, because she knew that her brother's decaying body would now emit an odor. Jesus said to her, "Did I not tell you that if you believed, you would see the glory of God?" (v. 40). Martha forgot the loving message that Jesus sent when He first heard the news of her brother's illness (v. 4). She thought that her brother's death put an end to that promise.

No matter what circumstances we experience, glorifying God is the most important responsibility we have. It's not important that you and I are comfortable, but it is important that God is glorified. When our Lord thought about His own suffering and death, He said, "The hour has come for the Son of Man to be glorified" (John 12:23). He didn't say "crucified," which would have been the natural thing to say, but "glorified." Jesus looked beyond the shame and pain of the cross to the glory He would bring to His Father. "I have brought you glory on earth by completing the work you gave me to do" (John 17:4).

Is it your prayer that God will be glorified in your life? I know there are times when we hurt and we're sure that we can't be comforted. There are times when we feel alone and we miss loved ones who have been taken home to be with the Lord. But keep in mind that God will be glorified if you commit yourself to Him and trust Him. He will be glorified in your life, and others will see His glory and come to trust Him. You will grow in your walk with the Lord and learn to trust Him more.

God will be glorified through your testimony. "Therefore many of the Jews who had come to visit Mary, and had seen what Jesus did, put their faith in him" (John 11:45).

69

Bereavement is a difficult burden to bear, but it's worth it all if other people come to know Jesus as their Savior.

God loves you. That's the first assurance you should claim. Christ is with you and you are not alone. God's will is best. You don't have to understand His will or be able to explain it. Don't live by explanations; live by promises. God's will is best, and God will be glorified if you trust Christ and obey His Word.

Jesus asked Martha, "Do you believe this?" and she replied, "Yes, Lord, I believe that you are the Christ, the Son of God, who was to come into the world" (vv. 26–27). If you believe in Jesus Christ, then death has no terror for you. If you believe in Jesus Christ, then you can have the comfort of God today. The loneliness of sorrow is conquered by the presence and power of the Lord Jesus Christ. Do you believe?

7

The Older Brother
THE LONELINESS OF STUBBORNNESS

The people of the village were joyful and having a wonderful time. The fatted calf had been killed and roasted, and the whole village was celebrating the homecoming of a wayward boy. Everybody was joyful except for one man—the boy's older brother. He was standing outside the house, angry and determined, refusing to go in and enjoy the feast. He was stubborn, and because he was stubborn, he was lonely. He might have called his attitude "conviction," but it was just old-fashioned stubbornness. He was angry because he was not getting his own way.

Think with me about the loneliness of stubbornly having your own way. Let's examine our own hearts in the light of Luke 15:25–32:

> "Meanwhile, the older son was in the field. When he came near the house, he heard music and dancing. So he called one of the servants and asked him what was going on. 'Your brother has come,' he replied, 'and your father has killed the fattened calf because he has him back safe and sound.' The older brother became angry and refused to go in. So

his father went out and pleaded with him. But he answered his father, 'Look! All these years I've been slaving for you and never disobeyed your orders. Yet you never gave me even a young goat so I could celebrate with my friends. But when this son of yours who has squandered your property with prostitutes comes home, you kill the fattened calf for him!' 'My son,' the father said, 'you are always with me, and everything I have is yours. But we had to celebrate and be glad, because this brother of yours was dead and is alive again; he was lost and is found.'"

Our Lord told this parable in order to describe two kinds of sinners—carnal worldly sinners and self-righteous religious sinners. The younger son (we call him "the prodigal son") is a picture of people who are guilty of the sins of the flesh. He wasted his substance in riotous living. But the older brother is a picture of those who are guilty of sins of the spirit, sins such as pride and criticism. Everybody could see the sins of the younger son, but they couldn't see the sins of his older brother. His sins were hidden in his heart until he opened his mouth and began to talk. The prodigal son was repentant and brokenhearted, but his older brother was stubborn and proud, and he was a lonely man.

The prodigal son is a picture of the tax collectors and sinners who gathered around the Lord Jesus to hear Him speak (Luke 15:1). The older brother is a picture of the Pharisees and the scribes, who were very good at criticizing others but not so good when it came to judging their own hearts. They criticized Jesus for fellowshipping with the irreligious crowd.

Many things were wrong with the older brother, but one defect was obvious—he was a stubborn man who wanted to have his own way. He was angry and would not forgive his younger brother and go in and enjoy the feast. People today do the same thing. Many families have members who are carrying a grudge or are angry at somebody for something that happened years ago. They won't attend family gatherings or even speak to their relatives because of some long-standing disagreement. Of all problems, family problems are the worst, and the devil likes to use them to create heartache and sorrow.

Ungrateful to Your Father

Let's consider the sad consequences of stubbornness. To begin with, notice how this son treats his father: He is ungrateful and disobedient. Stubbornness has a way of making us ungrateful because we insist on having our own way. Instead of being grateful for what we do have, we complain about what we don't have. "Lo, these many years I have worked for you, and you never even gave me a little goat so I could have a party for my friends. But let this son of yours come home, who has been wasting your money in wicked living, and for him you kill not a goat, but the best animal we have—the fattened calf." Families in that culture always kept such a calf ready for special occasions.

The older brother mistreated his father. He didn't even address his father politely (v. 29). In the East, you address your parents by saying "Father" or "Mother." But the older son started out with, "Look! All these years I've been slaving for you!" He wasn't even polite to his father, forcing his father to come outside and talk to him. He wouldn't go in and talk to his father. In his compassion for both boys, the father came outside, but it must have embarrassed him.

The older brother doubted his father's generosity. "All these years I've worked for you, and you've never given me anything!" (see v. 29). The father was a very generous man, yet the older boy treated his father like a cruel and selfish employer. Why hadn't he told his father that he wanted to have a party? He should have asked his father if he could invite some of his friends over for a feast. Surely the father would have let him do it—that is, *if* the older son had any friends.

When we're stubborn, we show that we're ungrateful. I think one of the best antidotes for loneliness is thankfulness to God for all He gives to us and does for us. Over and over in the Bible we're commanded to be thankful. No matter what the circumstances, we should be thankful to the Lord. I wonder if the older brother ever heard Psalm 100 read in the synagogue? "Shout for joy to the LORD, all the earth. Worship the LORD with gladness; come before him with joyful songs. . . . Give thanks to him and praise his name" (vv. 1–4). If he did hear it read, the message didn't penetrate his heart.

Are we ungrateful to our Father in heaven? All that He has is ours through Jesus Christ our Savior and Lord. That's an amazing truth! We are "heirs of God and co-heirs with Christ" (Rom. 8:17). You may be complaining today because of something you don't have or because of the way something happened; but stop to thank God for all He has given you and done for you. Don't be ungrateful to your Father.

Unhappy with Your Work

The older brother was mistreating his father, but he was also mistreating himself. He was making himself unhappy when he could have been rejoicing. This son looked like a model worker. He was obedient to his father. He was loyal. He worked hard in the field. It's possible for us to be working hard and doing the Father's work but not be close to the Father's heart. The older brother seemed like a model worker, but his heart was all wrong. He was a drudge. He was doing his job because he *had* to. Secretly, he was hoping to get something special, perhaps a big feast.

Many people carry a hidden agenda in their hearts. They do their work and take care of their family, but deep inside they have a hidden agenda. Sometimes you read in the newspaper about a well-known person who suddenly took off, left his wife and children (or her husband and children), and disappeared to start a new life. Why? Because for years he's been carrying this hidden agenda inside. He might be working in an office, but he really wants to go to some exotic place and paint pictures. Or he drives a truck, but what he really wants is to fly a plane. The older brother had a hidden agenda, and he finally admitted it.

Ephesians 6:6 tells us we should do the will of God "from the heart." The Bible says, "Delight yourself in the LORD and he will give you the desires of your heart" (Ps. 37:4). If I delight in the Lord, my desires will be the right desires— His desires. If my desire is to delight in the Lord and please Him, then He will give me what I delight in. But if my desires are selfish, then the Father will not answer.

The older brother had no joy in his labor, no enthusiasm, only drudgery. He wasn't serving from the heart. He did his work stubbornly, not happily. He was ungrateful to his father. He was unhappy in his own life.

Unforgiving toward Your Brother

The older boy had a bad relationship with his father, but he also had a bad relationship with his brother. He was unforgiving and unloving toward his younger brother. After all, the younger brother had taken his share of the inheritance and gone off to a far country, where he promptly wasted it. He lost everything. He ended up friendless, homeless, hungry, and homesick, a boy with a bad conscience. Finally he said, "I'm going home," and he returned to the father (see Luke 15:18).

Did you ever notice what convicted the younger son and convinced him to go home? It was the generosity of his father. "How many of my father's hired men have food to spare, and here I am starving to death!" (v. 17). It's the goodness of God that leads us to repentance (see Rom. 2:4). How strange that the older brother lived at home but didn't see his father's generosity, yet the younger brother far from home realized how good and generous his father really was.

You'd think that the older brother would have been watching for his brother to come home, but he wasn't. He didn't love his brother and didn't want him to come home. The older boy was in the field working when his brother came home. The father was watching for the prodigal, welcomed him, and had the servants kill the fatted calf and prepare a feast. The party was already in progress before the older brother found out what was going on. It's a sad thing when you don't know what's happening in your own family. Sometimes people in your family can be ill or in the hospital and you may not know about it. If we love one another, we keep in touch and share each other's joys and sorrows.

The older son wasn't watching for his brother's return. Why? Because he didn't *want* him to come back. He was glad the boy was gone. As long as the younger son was gone, the older son looked good. But when the boy came home and said, "Father, I'm sorry and I want to work for you," there was competition in the family.

The older son wouldn't even claim the boy was his brother, referring to him instead as "this son of yours" (Luke 15:30). Are there some people in God's family that you won't claim? Are you unloving toward your brothers and sisters in Christ? The older brother wouldn't talk to the younger boy, and he wouldn't go in and join the party. The father had to come out and talk to the older brother. This is the tragedy of stubbornness and wanting to have our own way: It poisons us with anger and criticism, it hurts God and other people, and it robs us of joyful fellowship.

Don't carry malice in your heart. Don't carry grudges. If you're going to have an enemy, get a good one, because an enemy is a very expensive thing. According to physicians, when we carry hatred inside, it can lead to headaches, backaches, ulcers, and heart trouble. Even worse, it will hurt your fellowship with God.

The younger brother was a threat to his older brother. As long as the boy was out sinning in the far country, the older brother looked good. As long as the younger brother was gone, the older brother had more authority in the home. But the father loved his younger son and was glad to have him back home. "Be kind and compassionate to one another, forgiving each other, just as in Christ God forgave you" (Eph. 4:32).

The older brother was building walls instead of bridges. He had built a wall between himself and his father, but he had also built walls between himself and his work and himself and his brother. He was a man who was ungrateful, unhappy, and unforgiving, a lonely man behind selfish walls of protection that shut out joyful fellowship.

Unloving toward Others

In one word, the older brother was unloving. One of the sad consequences of stubbornness is that it makes us keep everything inside. Our hearts get harder and harder and we find ourselves unable to reach out in love to those around us. We nurse our grudges, all the while poisoning ourselves.

It's interesting that this older brother had no problem talking to his father's servant. He would speak to a servant, but he wouldn't talk to his own brother. He also had a difficult time talking to his father. The older boy had not really experienced the forgiveness of God. You have to experience forgiveness before you can share forgiveness.

In Matthew 18 we read our Lord's parable about the king who audited his books and discovered that one of his servants owed him millions of dollars. So he called the servant in and said, "I'm going to sell you into slavery." The man fell down and begged the king to give him time to pay the bill. The king had compassion on the man and forgave him the huge debt. You'd think the man would have gone out and praised the Lord and been kind to everybody. But instead, he went out and found a fellow servant who owed him a few dollars. He said, "Pay me, or I'll put you in jail!" (see vv. 28–30). The servant said, "Please, give me time," but he was thrown in jail. When the king heard about it, he said, "This is wrong. I forgave you a great debt. Couldn't you forgive your fellow servant the small debt he owed you?" And the king put the man in prison. Jesus said, "This is what your Father will do to you if you don't forgive your brother from your heart" (see v. 35).

When you experience God's forgiveness, you have no problem sharing God's forgiveness. This is the message our Lord was trying to get across to the Pharisees. The Pharisees were proud, self-righteous, moral, upstanding people. They were religious people. They tithed and prayed and were very careful about practicing their religion. But they had not really experienced God's forgiveness in their hearts.

The older brother lacked the fruit of the Spirit. He didn't show any love to his brother or to his father. He had no joy in his life. He was a drudge. He went to work every day and slaved because he had to. He had no peace. He was causing a family feud! Long-suffering? Of course not! He had no patience with anybody. He lost his temper and was angry. Gentleness? Anything but! He was very hard on his father and his younger brother. He lacked goodness and faith. Why didn't he believe what his father said? Why didn't he act on his father's word? He was a man who was very unloving toward those around him.

What he really needed was salvation. That was the message Jesus was trying to get across. The publicans and sinners knew they were lost; they knew they had to trust Jesus. The Pharisees and scribes thought, "We don't need to be saved. We're righteous." Our Lord was saying to them, "But you're just the opposite. You *desperately* need salvation!"

We have learned from the older brother that stubbornness—wanting to have our own way—leads to loneliness. If we harbor ill will in our hearts, if we harbor malice and carry grudges, we will be very lonely people. We will end up being ungrateful to our heavenly Father, unhappy with our work, unforgiving toward others, and unloving toward those around us. Stubbornness has a way of robbing us of the things that really count—the Father's fellowship, the love of our family, enjoyment with others. The loneliness of stubbornness is one of the worst kinds of loneliness.

Are you on the outside, or are you inside the fellowship enjoying the party? Is everybody else enjoying the Father's fellowship while you stand outside? Is everybody else enjoying fellowship with one another while you are lonely? Why are you on the outside? Is it because you are stubborn? Is it because you refuse to submit to God? My plea is that you confess your sins to the Lord and to those you have hurt, and humbly accept God's forgiveness. Then start to enjoy the feast! The Father prepared it with you in mind.

8

Jesus Christ
THE ANSWER TO LONELINESS

In the previous chapters we have met seven different people and discovered six different kinds of loneliness. The loneliness of sin was seen in the life of Cain. In Job, we discovered the loneliness of suffering. Moses taught us about the loneliness of service, and Elijah warned us against the loneliness of self-pity. Mary and Martha taught us how to have comfort in the loneliness of sorrow. The older brother warned us about the loneliness of stubbornness and wanting our own way. The final and complete answer to all loneliness is faith in Jesus Christ. He is the answer to loneliness in your life.

Loneliness has been defined in many different ways. My own definition is this: Loneliness is the malnutrition of the soul that results from living on substitutes.

> Come, all you who are thirsty, come to the waters; and you who have no money, come, buy and eat! Come, buy wine and milk without money and without cost. Why spend money on what is not bread, and your labor on what does

not satisfy? Listen, listen to me and eat what is good, and
your soul will delight in the richest of fare. Give ear and
come to me; hear me, that your soul may live.

Isaiah 55:1–3

That's God's invitation to everyone who is lonely. God
asks us, "Why are you living on substitutes when you can
have true, lasting blessings through faith in Jesus Christ?"

Let's take each of the lonely people we have studied and
ask ourselves this question: What message would the Lord
Jesus Christ give to each of them? What message would the
Lord Jesus Christ give to Cain or to Job or to the older
brother? These would certainly be messages that you and I
need to hear.

Christ Can Forgive You

Let's begin with Cain and the loneliness of sin. I believe
the message the Lord Jesus Christ would give to Cain is
found in John 14:6—"I am the way and the truth and the
life. No one comes to the Father except through me." Jesus
said, "I am the way." The tragedy is that Cain had his own
way. Jude 11 talks about "the way of Cain." What is the way
of Cain? It's the way of religion without faith. It's the way of
self-righteousness without the blood sacrifice of Jesus Christ,
the Lamb of God. It's the way of doing your best with what
you have but not trusting in the Lord Jesus Christ. Jesus
would say to Cain, "I am the way." If you ever hope to
approach God, you must come through the Lord Jesus
Christ.

Someone may say, "That sounds very exclusive! Aren't all
religions the same? Don't all religions lead us to God as long
as we are sincere?" No, they don't. "Salvation is found in no
one else, for there is no other name under heaven given to

81

men by which we must be saved" (Acts 4:12). Cain had his own way, but Jesus said, "I am the way."

Jesus also said, "I am the truth." Cain, you will remember, was a liar. He lied to his brother and he lied to God. Although he worshiped with his brother, he had murder in his heart. Cain lied to God: "Am I my brother's keeper?" (Gen. 4:9). He lied to himself and convinced himself he could sin and get away with it. The reason many people are lonely is because they will not face the truth. Jesus said, "Then you will know the truth, and the truth will set you free" (John 8:32).

Cain was a murderer, but Jesus said, "I am the life." Cain murdered his brother, but in reality he murdered himself. He committed spiritual suicide by lying to God and murdering his brother.

Only Jesus Christ can save us. If you want eternal life, it has to come through Him. Cain was a child of the devil. First John 3:12 informs us that he was "of that wicked one." John 8:44 reminds us that Satan is a liar and a murderer. Cain was also a liar and a murderer, born of the wicked one.

Cain tried to solve his problems by building a city and living on substitutes. He carried his guilt with him. Jesus would say to Cain, as He says to us today, "I can forgive your sin. I can take away your guilt. I can give you a new beginning. I am the way, the truth, and the life; no one comes to the Father except through me." If you are experiencing the loneliness of sin, that's the message you need.

God Is in Control

What message would the Lord Jesus give to Job, who suffered so much? I think He would say to Job what He said to Peter and the apostles in Luke 22:31–32: "Simon, Simon,

Satan has asked to sift you [plural; all of the disciples] as wheat. But I have prayed for you, Simon, that your faith may not fail. And when you have turned back, strengthen your brothers."

Job didn't know that Satan and the Lord God were talking about him up in heaven. Job did not know what was going on behind the scenes. It was important that Job *not* understand what was going on, because he had to learn to trust God without explanations. But these verses tell us that God is in control, not Satan. The sovereignty of God is so great that He can allow Satan to do his worst and still bring about His best. These words remind us that our suffering is working for us and not against us, because God is in control.

Our Lord said that the experience of suffering is like the sifting of wheat. Why would a farmer sift wheat? To get rid of the chaff. Why does God permit Satan to attack us? Why does He allow us to go through suffering? To sift us, to take out of our lives those things that are cheap and useless and to put into our lives those things that are good and lasting.

Our Lord said to Peter, "I have prayed for you." The Lord Jesus upholds us in the furnace of affliction and stands with us and prays for us. Yes, God is in control. Suffering works for us because Jesus Christ upholds us and is praying for us in heaven. The result of all this is that God ministers through us to other people. "When you have turned back, strengthen your brothers."

God did turn Peter back, forgave him, and helped him to strengthen others. In fact, one of the major themes of Peter's first letter is that suffering can lead to glory if we submit to the Lord.

If you are suffering today, remember that God, not Satan, is in control, and that your suffering can work for you because Jesus is in heaven praying for you. Your suffering can equip you to effectively minister to others because you too have experienced the grace of God.

Christ Wants to Share Your Burden

What message would the Lord Jesus Christ give to Moses? You'll remember how distraught and frustrated Moses was because the burden of leading the nation of Israel was too heavy for him. The work that he had to do was too demanding. The people were so ungrateful that Moses wanted to die.

I think the message that Jesus would give to Moses is found in Matthew 11:28–30: "Come to me, all you who are weary and burdened, and I will give you rest. Take my yoke upon you and learn from me, for I am gentle and humble in heart, and you will find rest for your souls. For my yoke is easy and my burden is light."

Moses was frustrated and was feeling the weight of his burdens because he thought he had to carry the load himself. All of God's people, and especially God's servants, need to remember that the Lord Jesus Christ wants to carry the burdens with you. We all say, "I have so many things to do and I can't accomplish them all!" We need to rely on the Lord Jesus Christ, for He said, "Apart from me, you can do nothing" (John 15:5).

The Lord doesn't offer us rest *from* life but rest *in* life. He's not saying, "I'll take away your responsibilities so you will never have to worry about bearing burdens." That, to me, would not be a very happy life. I want to be involved in service. I want to be busy serving God the best I can. Paul wrote, "For each one should carry his own load" (Gal. 6:5). Christ assures us that, with His strength, we can carry the burdens and responsibilities of life and still have peace in our hearts.

He's not talking about escape from life but divine enablement in life. This is the way we build Christian character.

When we come to Christ, we stop looking to ourselves and our circumstances for the help we need, and we start looking to the Lord. When we take His yoke, we accept the tasks He's chosen for us and not the work everybody else wants us to do. We don't feel that we have to do everything, but only those things Jesus selects for us. We spend time every day learning about Jesus and getting closer to His heart, and we find rest for our souls.

The yoke that Jesus gives us is tailor-made for us. He knows exactly how we feel, what we can do, and how much we can take. But even more, He is yoked with us so that we do things together with our Lord. *Together* we teach a Sunday school class or lead the choir or direct a missionary endeavor. Yoked together with Christ, parents raise their precious children and pastors care for God's people. Because we are yoked with the Lord Jesus, we can carry burdens and still have rest in our hearts.

Serve Christ Rather Than Self

What would the Lord Jesus say to Elijah, who was filled with self-pity and wanted to die? I think the words of John 12:23–28 apply to Elijah's case:

> Jesus replied, "The hour has come for the Son of Man to be glorified. I tell you the truth, unless a kernel of wheat falls to the ground and dies, it remains only a single seed. But if it dies, it produces many seeds. The man who loves his life will lose it, while the man who hates his life in this world will keep it for eternal life. Whoever serves me must follow me; and where I am, there my servant also will be. My Father will honor the one who serves me. Now my heart is

troubled, and what shall I say? 'Father, save me from this hour'? No, it was for this very reason I came to this hour. Father, glorify your name!"

The contrasts our Lord presents here are very striking. We are either going to love our lives or lose our lives for Jesus' sake. If you love your own life and try to take care of only yourself, you will lose your life. But if you lose your life for the sake of Jesus, you will save it. Either you will serve yourself or you will serve God and others. Either you will run away and do your own thing or you will follow Christ, even to the cross. You will be either lonely or fruitful. You will pray "Father, save me!" or "Father, glorify your name!"

You may be serving the Lord today and feel like quitting. Please don't wallow in self-pity. Lose your life for Jesus' sake. Serve God, not your own feelings. Follow Christ, even if it means crucifixion. You don't want to be alone. The loneliness of self-pity is tragic. You want to be fruitful. Let God plant you where He wants you, and you will bear fruit for His glory.

Christ Has Conquered Death

What would our Lord Jesus Christ say to Mary and Martha as they were experiencing the loneliness of sorrow? Exactly what He *did* say: "I am the resurrection and the life. He who believes in me will live, even though he dies; and whosoever lives and believes in me will never die. Do you believe this?" (John 11:25–26).

It isn't enough to believe in a doctrine written in a book, even if that book is the Bible. We must have a living relationship with a person—Jesus Christ—the one the Bible speaks about. Martha believed in the doctrine of the resurrection and said, "I know he will rise again in the resurrection at the last day" (v. 24). But Jesus assured her that she didn't have to wait until the last day for that to happen. Wherever Jesus is, there you will have resurrection and life. Jesus is the fulfillment of God's promises (see 2 Cor. 1:20). Wherever Jesus is, God's power is available for the promise to be fulfilled.

As we go through the loneliness of sorrow, we have Jesus at our side. We have the assurance of resurrection power. We have His abundant life. Those who die in Christ go to be with Him, and one day He will raise them. Those who are alive when He returns will never die. He asks, "Do you believe this?" You say, "Yes, I do believe." Then you can go through sorrow and not break down, because Jesus Christ is the Resurrection and the Life.

It's not enough that we simply believe a doctrine. We must be vitally related to the person who has conquered death, Jesus Christ.

Forgive As Christ Forgave

Finally, what would our Lord Jesus Christ say to the older brother? I believe that His words in Matthew 6 would apply to the older brother: "Forgive us our debts, as we also have forgiven our debtors. . . . For if you forgive men when they sin against you, your heavenly Father will also forgive you. But if you do not forgive men their sins, your Father will not forgive your sins" (vv. 12, 14–15).

The older brother was lonely because he was stubborn and would not forgive his father or his younger brother. Forgiveness is a bridge that we all must cross at one time or another. You may say, "I won't forgive my brother because he doesn't deserve it!" But someday he may have to forgive you, and then what will you do? Nobody deserves forgiveness, but God forgives us because of His grace through Jesus Christ.

Our Lord isn't suggesting that we're saved by forgiving other people. We're saved through faith in Jesus Christ. But if we have experienced God's forgiveness, we will want to forgive others and heed Paul's admonition to "be kind and compassionate to one another, forgiving each other, just as in Christ God forgave you" (Eph. 4:32).

These then are the messages Jesus would give to these people. If you are lonely today because of sin, He can forgive you. If you are lonely because of suffering, He can give you grace and strength. If you are lonely in your service, take His yoke, do His work, and receive His rest. If you are lonely because of self-pity, give your life to Him in submission. In losing your life, you will save it. If you are in the loneliness of sorrow, Jesus will give you comfort. If you are in the loneliness of stubbornness, He will help you to forgive and love others.

Don't be lonely today. Let Jesus change your life.

9

The Comforter

Before Jesus went to the cross to die for the sins of the world, He met with His disciples in an upper room and taught them how to live for Him and serve Him in His absence. He was returning to the Father and they would no longer have His physical presence with them. This would be a new experience for them, because they had depended on Him for everything. But it was necessary for Jesus to return to the Father so He could send the Holy Spirit—the Comforter or Counselor—who would take His place and do for them all that He had done. Jesus had been *with* His disciples, but the Spirit would be *in* them and would remain with them (John 14:16–17).

Different New Testament translations use different words for the Greek word *paraklete* found in the original text. The word simply means "one called alongside." Some translate it as helper, others as counselor or comforter. It may even be translated as intercessor, advocate, or pleader. If you keep in mind the original meaning of "comfort" you will better understand how the Holy Spirit helps God's children in times of loneliness and discouragement. "Comfort" comes from two Latin words—*cum,* meaning "with," and *fortis,* meaning "strength." When the Holy Spirit works in our lives, He gives us the strength we need to live for Christ, serve Him, and overcome whatever obstacles stand in the way.

But the Comforter doesn't work in a vacuum, nor does He work without specific purposes. He ministers according to certain basic principles, and if we understand them and apply them, the Spirit will work on our behalf and give us strength. Jesus didn't send the Spirit as a luxury for us to enjoy so that we can become super saints, but as an intimate friend to assist us in every aspect of life and ministry.

The Holy Spirit Glorifies Jesus Christ

Jesus said, "He [the Comforter] will bring glory to me by taking from what is mine and making it known to you" (John 16:14). It's tragic when people want the Holy Spirit to glorify them and call attention to their virtues and achievements. If we call attention to ourselves instead of to Jesus Christ, then it isn't the Spirit who is at work in our lives. One of the problems Paul had with the believers at Corinth was the egotistical display of their spiritual gifts. What they did wasn't for the edification of the church or the glorification of the Lord, but for the exaltation of the believers.

During our times of loneliness, the Holy Spirit is with us, and He wants to use our situation to glorify Christ. If all we do is feel sorry for ourselves and complain, then the Spirit can't work in us and through us. No matter how painful and difficult our lives might be, the Spirit can still use us to bring glory to Jesus Christ and to influence others to trust Him. We can join the apostle Paul and say, "Now I want you to know . . . that what has happened to me has really served to advance the gospel" (Phil. 1:12).

The Holy Spirit longs to make us more like Christ and to glorify Him, not in spite of our problems, but because of them. Like Paul, our desire should be "that now as always Christ will be exalted in my body, whether by life or by death" (Phil. 1:20). If we center our attention on ourselves, we will make the situation worse; but if we focus on glorifying Christ, the Spirit will make the situation better by making us better Christians.

During my years of pastoral ministry, I visited many sick and afflicted people, and I can testify that there's a vast difference when the Spirit is in control. Walking into some sickrooms was like entering a lion's cage, while the atmosphere in other rooms was like that of the Holy of Holies. What made the difference? In some rooms, the people allowed the Holy Spirit the freedom to glorify Christ. In other rooms, the Spirit was grieved by anger, complaining, and unbelief.

The Holy Spirit Teaches Us the Word

Jesus said, "But when he, the Spirit of truth, comes, he will guide you into all truth" (John 16:13). The believers in the early church had the Old Testament and the oral traditions about Jesus that were treasured and repeated and ultimately written down. The Holy Spirit reminded them of what Jesus had said (John 14:26), and He reminds us as well if we take time to read the Word and meditate on it. To see Jesus Christ in the Scriptures and to allow the Spirit to write His Word upon our minds and hearts is one of the surest cures for loneliness. This involves not just Bible study, as good as that is, but feeding on the Word, rejoicing in it, and receiving its nourishment and strength by faith.

The eminent British preacher Charles Haddon Spurgeon said, "Many a text is written in a secret ink which must be held to the fire of adversity to make it visible." When the children of this world are disappointed and depressed, they look for some kind of distraction and turn on the television set. But the people of God don't want shallow entertainment; they want the rich enlightenment and enablement of the Word of God. "He sent forth his word and healed them" (Ps. 107:20).

I recall times in my life and ministry when everything looked very discouraging and it seemed as though my work was in vain. Then, in the course of my daily devotional time, a promise from the Word would leap out at me and send sunshine through the darkness. I could say with Jeremiah, "When your words came, I ate them; they were my joy and my heart's delight" (Jer. 15:16).

The Spirit of God came to glorify Christ, and He uses the Word to accomplish that ministry. As we see Christ in the Scriptures, our hearts are encouraged and we find new life and hope even in the midst of difficulties. To quote Spurgeon again, "Our griefs are often waves which wash us to the Rock."

We live by promises, not by explanations. No matter how we feel, no matter what we see, no matter how we think people are treating us, no matter how we may question God, the promises of the Lord never change and never fail. "You know with all your heart and soul that not one of all the good promises the LORD your God gave you has failed. Every promise has been fulfilled; not one has failed" (Josh. 23:14).

The Holy Spirit Assists Us When We Pray

Paul wrote, "We do not know what we ought to pray for, but the Spirit himself intercedes for us with groans that words cannot express. And he who searches our hearts knows the mind of the Spirit, because the Spirit intercedes for the saints in accordance with God's will" (Rom. 8:26–27).

If you are a child of God, then at this very moment Jesus Christ is interceding for you at the throne of the Father (Rom. 8:34). He represents us before the Father and presents our petitions to Him. When we pray, the Holy Spirit takes our requests and causes them to agree with the will of God. Both the Holy Spirit and the Son know God's will for your life; they understand the Father's purpose is to conform His children "to the likeness of his Son" (Rom. 8:29).

It's God's will that His children "rejoice in the Lord" (Phil. 3:1) and "do everything without complaining or arguing" (Phil. 2:14). The Holy Spirit who wrote the Word knows this perfectly. If my heart is heavy because circumstances and people distress me, I need to unite with my Intercessors—the Son of God and the Spirit of God—and seek to pray the will of God. Of course, the Spirit will guide us through the Word, so it's important that the Word abide in our hearts (John 15:7). Quietly meditating on the Word, submissively praying to the Lord, and lovingly communing with the Savior will quiet the feverish spirit, calm the troubled mind, and help control the hasty tongue.

I like to pray the Lord's Word back to Him. I use the Lord's Prayer each morning in my personal prayer time, but I also use the inspired prayers of Scripture, applying them to my personal situation. When we're in touch with the Lord in heaven and the Spirit within us, and when the Lord is speaking to us through His Word, how can we be lonely? We never need to fear the will of God, because the will of God comes from the loving heart of God (Ps. 33:11). "This poor man called, and the LORD heard him; he saved him out of all his troubles" (Ps. 34:6).

Let the Spirit of God transform your loneliness into solitude, and enjoy a time of quiet fellowship with the Lord. Loneliness feeds on self-pity and self-centered thinking, and it tears us down; but solitude rejoices in seeing the Lord by faith and worshiping Him.

The Holy Spirit Empowers Us to Witness

Jesus said, "But you will receive power when the Holy Spirit comes on you; and you will be my witnesses" (Acts 1:8).

The only time I was a witness in court, the judge didn't ask me what I thought or how I felt. He asked me what I knew. Jesus didn't promise that we would feel like witnessing but that we would bear witness of who Jesus is and what He means to us. We are witnesses, not prosecuting attorneys, telling people that Jesus is alive and able to transform their lives if they will trust Him. But if our lives don't back up that message, we'd better keep quiet.

When you find a time of loneliness creeping up on you, you have to make a decision: Am I going to use this experience to witness for Christ or to gather sympathy for myself? Am I going to reach for the phone and burden somebody else with the way I feel, or am I going to pray, "Lord, whatever comes, help me to be a witness for Christ"? As the Lord enables us, we can overcome our self-centered thinking and begin to tell others about Jesus Christ. If I deliberately draw attention to myself and my trials, I'm not a witness for Christ; but if I praise the Lord in the midst of emotional pain, I will find that the Holy Spirit uses praise to change things. "Hallelujah—praise the Lord!" is wonderful medicine for a discouraged heart.

We can't do this alone, and the more we try, the worse the situation will become. We need the empowering of the

Spirit and the fullness of the Spirit. This we receive by faith in response to His command, "Be filled with the Spirit" (Eph. 5:18), for His commandments are His enablements.

The Holy Spirit Produces His Fruit in Our Lives

Paul wrote, "But the fruit of the Spirit is love, joy, peace, patience, kindness, goodness, faithfulness, gentleness and self-control" (Gal. 5:22–23). Can you imagine any child of God having these blessings and yet experiencing loneliness?

Loneliness is often a form of selfishness, and the answer to selfishness is love. When the love of Christ is "poured out" in our hearts by the Holy Spirit (Rom. 5:5), the fruit of the Spirit begins to appear, starting with love. When love is lifted upward to the Lord, it produces joy, and love and joy in the heart bring peace. When we have the peace of God, we experience patience and kindness, two qualities that help us get along with other people. Instead of insisting that they help us, we insist that they allow us to help them. As we cultivate a loving heart and allow the Spirit to control us, we see the garden of God's grace produce a harvest of fruit that feeds others and makes their way easier. A pastor friend of mine, who is now in heaven, used to pray every day, "Father, help me today not to add to anybody's problems." I'm sure the Holy Spirit enjoyed answering that prayer!

The Holy Spirit is always with us. We can draw upon His life by faith and discover how adequate He is for every situation. But it's important that we cultivate the fruit of the Spirit, for it takes time to produce the kind of harvest we need. You can grow mushrooms overnight, but it takes time to produce fruit. When we lie to the Holy Spirit by pretending to be more spiritual than we really are (Acts 5:1–11), or grieve the Spirit by harboring sins that ought to be confessed and forsaken (Eph. 4:30–32), or quench the Spirit by deliberately rebelling against God's will (1 Thess. 5:19), then we can't cultivate the fruit of the Spirit. Life becomes barren.

"Since we live by the Spirit, let us keep in step with the Spirit" (Gal. 5:25). That means we don't lag behind and we don't run ahead. "Do not be like the horse [impatient and impulsive] or the mule [stubborn]" (Ps. 32:9), but be like the obedient sheep who listens to the shepherd's voice and stays close to the shepherd's side.

10

The People of God

We've already learned that there's a difference between loneliness and solitude. You can be in a stadium full of cheering football fans or in a pressing crowd at a Christmas sale and still feel very lonely. But you can be all by yourself and not feel lonely. We all need occasional times of solitude because they create margins in our lives and give us room for growth. The philosopher George Santayana said, "Society is like the air, necessary to breathe, but insufficient to live on." When society becomes smothering, we need to withdraw for a time and charge our spiritual and emotional batteries.

On January 1, 1850, American naturalist Henry David Thoreau wrote to his friend Harrison Blake, "I have lately got back to that glorious society called Solitude." Whenever I reread Thoreau's *Walden,* I smile at his statement in chapter 5: "I have a great deal of company in my house; especially in the morning, when nobody calls." Thoreau lived in his little house at Walden Pond for two years, two months, and two days, but in spite of what he wrote about his love of solitude, he didn't completely abandon society. He frequently walked to nearby Concord to visit his family and friends, and occasionally he would take long walks with like-minded companions and chat about mutual interests.

"It is not good for the man to be alone" (Gen. 2:18). This tells us something about life in general, not just about marriage. People need each other. Granted, some people are introverts and prefer to be alone, while others are extroverts and can't live without frequently rubbing shoulders with a crowd at the mall or gathering at a friend's house. History reports the words and deeds of the desert fathers who lived alone in caves and learned much about God. But for most of us, whether we're introverts, extroverts, or a little of each, when it comes to life, we can't successfully make it alone.

As followers of Jesus Christ, we're part of a great fellowship that transcends time and space, a fellowship that Paul called "his whole family in heaven and on earth" (Eph. 3:15). Millions of people around the world pray "Our Father" and not "My Father" because they're members of a fantastic fellowship called the church of Jesus Christ. The church is not a denomination, but an incredible group of people who own Jesus Christ as Lord and seek to live for Him. As part of this wonderful spiritual fellowship, we ought to be able to find the resources we need to overcome persistent and painful loneliness.

The Nomads

Of all the lonely people I've met during my years of pastoral ministry, the most miserable were professed Christians who had turned their backs on the family of God and stopped participating in the life and worship of a local church. I began to call them "the nomads"—they'd get mad, say no, and off they'd go! They were the people who shopped around and visited church after church. Eventually, they stopped doing even that and just stayed home. To be sure, they could give reasons—or excuses—for their disobedience to Hebrews 10:19–25 and our Lord's frequent admonition that we love one another, but they didn't sound very convincing.

These unhappy souls were imperfect people looking for a perfect church, but they couldn't find one. There are none. By "perfect," of course, they meant a church that pleased them. They could find something wrong with every church they visited and would use that defect as an excuse for going elsewhere. But the longer I was in ministry, the better I understood that these people abandoned ship, not because the boat was sinking, but because they didn't know how to swim. The longer they stayed in a church and the better people got to know them, the more frightened they became that somebody would discover the truth about them. As visitors, they came across as mature, vibrant Christians, but when you got to know them, you discovered how shallow they were.

The scenario was repeated in church after church. The first few months they attended any given church, the services were just wonderful and the people friendly. "We have finally found the church we've been looking for!" was their enthusiastic report, but then things began to change. Somebody would approach them about being part of a weekly Bible study, and they would begin to back off. Somebody else would ask if they could assist in ushering or perhaps sing in the choir, and they would back further off. By the time the pastor got around to visiting their home, they were totally turned off and asked to be left alone. "We don't want to be bothered"—as if serving the Lord is a bother!

Truth and Love

People who have difficulty being lovingly open and honest, who wear masks, play roles, and are afraid to take risks, rarely build lasting friendships or get involved in team activities. They want to be left alone to brood over the hypocrisy in the churches and bask in the warmth of their own spirituality. I soon discovered that it was futile to discuss the matter with them because their minds and hearts were closed. They couldn't face the truth because they didn't understand Christian love. Maybe they weren't even Christians at all.

Churches and individual Christians mature in the Lord when they're part of a fellowship that understands and practices "speaking the truth in love" (Eph. 4:15). The same principle applies to families. Truth without love becomes brutality, and love without truth becomes hypocrisy. You can't build with those tools. But when truth and love are brought together, as they are in Jesus Christ, then the Spirit can work and build a dynamic and healthy fellowship. "Knowledge puffs up, but love builds up" (1 Cor. 8:1).

Christian love doesn't close its eyes to reality and pretend that every church is a Garden of Eden. Paul prayed that the love of the believers in Philippi might "abound more and more in knowledge and depth of insight" (Phil. 1:9). Christian love is not blind. But knowing the truth about ourselves and others should not prevent us from receiving one another and helping one another. When you read Paul's epistles, you learn very quickly that the saints in the early church were far from perfect; but Paul urged them to love one another, pray for one another, serve one another, and forgive one another.

No family is perfect, no army is perfect, and no body is perfect. But even imperfect families can raise healthy, normal children, and imperfect armies can win battles. Our bodies seem to develop more and more problems as we grow older, but we accept these painful changes, adjust to them, compensate for them, and do the best we can. That's the mature way to face life. That's the mature way to face the local church.

Love in Action

We need other people. They help us better understand ourselves, and they challenge us to discover and develop our gifts so we can serve others. Every image of the church in the New Testament speaks of togetherness. We are children in the same family, sheep in the same flock, soldiers in the same army, branches of the same vine, and members of the same body. We belong to each other, we affect each other, and we need each other. Any professed Christians who knowingly go against that basic spiritual principle are declaring that they've never truly been born again or that they've not taken time to learn the ABCs of the Christian life.

I grew up attending Sunday school and church and was converted to Christ a few days short of my sixteenth birthday. When I stood up during a midweek service and told the folks (many of them relatives) that I'd been saved and also that I felt a call to ministry, they immediately rallied around me and encouraged me—and put me to work. Within a few weeks, I was giving my testimony at the Saturday evening street meeting. Then they asked me to help in Vacation Bible School. The youth group attended Youth for Christ rallies, and I was asked to make sure there was a YFC poster on the high school bulletin board.

After I graduated from high school, I began to attend another church. Those dear people drafted me to teach a Sunday school class and preach in rescue missions. Why mention these things? Because it was the love and encouragement of the people in local churches that helped me discover and develop the spiritual gifts God had given me.

I was so busy for the Lord that I didn't have time to sit alone and feel sorry for myself. Whenever I did have a problem, I knew there were people in the church family who would be happy to talk with me, counsel me, and pray for me. Some of them even invited me home for Sunday dinner!

When we're depressed or discouraged, it's dangerous to be alone. When we keep our burdens to ourselves and don't humbly share them with others, those feelings go deeper and get worse. Even our Lord asked Peter, James, and John to pray with Him in the garden as He faced His hour of crisis. David was a gifted man, but he would never have succeeded without the help of others. He wrote, "As for the saints who are in the land, they are the glorious ones in whom is all my delight" (Ps. 16:3). No Christian is perfect, and some are very difficult to get along with; but all of us need each other. We can't make it alone. Trying to raise one Christian is like trying to raise one bee.

God wants His children to experience balanced growth—truth and love, knowledge and grace (2 Peter 3:18). If you study your Bible, read good books, and listen to media preachers, you can be an isolated saint and grow in knowledge, but you will never really grow in grace. To grow in grace requires other people. Just as it takes a diamond to cut a diamond, so it takes other believers to polish us and equip us. The differences we have with each other and the problems those differences create in the church family help us learn to speak the truth in love and pray our way into unity.

Big Brother Is a Bad Example

In a previous chapter, we considered the loneliness of the prodigal son's older brother, the self-righteous man who stayed outside the family and the feast (Luke 15:25–32). To me, the older brother is an example of the kind of person I've been writing about in this chapter. He couldn't enter into the joy of his brother's return because he didn't love his brother and didn't want him to return. His father even left the table to go out and plead with him to come in, something fathers in Eastern cultures would never do. In the parable, Jesus doesn't tell us if the son repented, forgave his brother, and came in to enjoy the feast. The story is left open ended, and we have to provide the conclusion according to our own convictions. The Book of Jonah is similar, and the older brother was a lot like Jonah.

There's no reason for any of us to be lonely when there's a church nearby where we can love others and they can love us. We all need a circle of praying friends. We all need an inner circle of people who will speak the truth in love and help us grow in grace, and for whom we can perform the same service. Take a concordance and a Bible and make a list of the "one another" statements in the New Testament and see what you're missing when you stay home by yourself. Here are just a few:

Be devoted to one another—Romans 12:10

Accept one another—Romans 15:7

Instruct one another—Romans 15:14

Have equal concern for each other—1 Corinthians 12:25

Carry each other's burdens—Galatians 6:2

Encourage one another—1 Thessalonians 5:11

Pray for each other—James 5:16

Offer hospitality to one another—1 Peter 4:9

When I began my ministry over fifty years ago, the church I pastored ended every communion service by singing "Blest Be the Tie That Binds." The song is almost forgotten today, but it's worth reviving.

Blest be the tie that binds
Our hearts in Christian love;
The fellowship of kindred minds
Is like to that above.

Before our Father's throne
We pour our ardent prayers;
Our fears, our hopes, our aims are one,
Our comforts and our cares.

We share our mutual woes,
Our mutual burdens bear;
And often for each other flows
The sympathizing tear.

When we asunder part,
It gives us inward pain;
But we shall still be joined in heart,
And hope to meet again.

John Fawcett

11

Memory, Mortality, and Mercy

During the years I served as a pastor, I was frequently called upon to conduct funeral services during the Christmas season, and it was never easy. The joy of Advent has a way of magnifying grief, especially if the deceased was a child or the parent of a young family. My own mother died shortly before Christmas in 1972, and celebrating Christmas that year made us feel her absence even more. If a suicide wants to cast a permanent shadow over the happiness of family and friends, he or she will choose a significant day on which to end his or her life—a family birthday, a wedding anniversary, or Christmas Day, for example. This usually gives more pain to those who are left behind, pain that is felt annually as that special day approaches.

Even beyond its practical and necessary uses in everyday life, memory is one of God's special gifts to us. It helps us to create family and recognize our roots in the past. It helps us to possess a personal history and an identity, without which we would be nonentities. But memory can also bring pain and loneliness, especially when we think about those who are gone or mistakes we've made or sins we've committed— sins that are confessed and forgiven but not yet forgotten.

Calling to mind loved ones who have died reminds us that we too will die, and the thought of this may bring a pall of loneliness over our lives.

Painful memories from the past and the anticipation of death at some unknown time in the future can bring seasons of painful loneliness, even to those who follow Jesus Christ and have no fear of death.

The Shadows of Past Sins

After finishing a radio broadcast one day, I was told I had an important telephone call that couldn't be delayed or turned over to anybody else. The caller turned out to be a very articulate Christian lady who had heard my radio message about the cleansing and healing power of Jesus Christ.

"When I was sixteen years old," she said quietly, "I did something I shouldn't have done—it was a sin—and it's haunted me ever since. I've confessed it to the Lord and I'm sure He's forgiven me, but why can't I escape the memory of that sin? My pastor wants me to teach a Sunday school class, but I don't think I'm worthy."

We read some Scriptures together as I explained what it means for God to "remember our sins no more" (Heb. 10:10–18). It means that He no longer holds them against us, that He treats us as though we had never sinned. If the memory of the sin humbles us and makes us turn to the Lord with thanksgiving for His mercies, then the memory does us good. But if remembering the past upsets us and hides the smile of God's face, then it's Satan, the accuser, who is attacking us. Then I read Romans 8:31–39 and encouraged her to rejoice in the truth that nothing can separate her from God's love. We prayed together, she thanked me, and the conversation was over.

Yes, there are painful consequences to forgiven sin, but we need not experience these consequences over and over again and live under a cloud of isolating guilt and fear. That isn't what it means to live in God's grace and walk in newness of life (see Rom. 6:4, 14). The prodigal's father forgave the boy and sealed that forgiveness with a new robe and a ring. Only the boy's older brother brought up his past conduct, but the father wouldn't listen to it.

Paul never forgot what kind of sinner he was before he met Jesus Christ (Acts 22:20; 1 Tim. 1:12–17), but he never allowed those memories to imprison him. He had experienced the grace of God. He had trusted the Savior and been forgiven. Even as he wrote about his painful past, he felt the love of God in his heart. The memory of his past sins humbled Paul, but it didn't cripple him.

The apostle Peter denied the Lord three times, but when he preached his second sermon, he accused the Jews of the same sin. "But you disowned [denied] the Holy and Righteous One!" (Acts 3:14). How could he do such a thing? Because he had met with the Lord, confessed his sins, and received forgiveness. When Jesus said to him, "Follow me," Peter was reinstated in his discipleship (see John 21:15–19). It was all of grace.

If the shadow of past sins—whether sins of commission or sins of omission—falls across your mind, or if you're called upon to encourage somebody in that condition, don't deny that the sin occurred or that the memory hurts. But do affirm that the blood of Jesus Christ is adequate to wash away the stain. Bathe yourself in the Word of God by reading passages such as Psalm 51, 1 John 1:5–2:2, Romans 8, Psalm 103, Hebrews 10, Romans 5, Isaiah 55, Micah 7:18–20, and Ephesians 1. Make much of the cross. It's the divinely appointed balm for troubled minds and broken hearts.

The Shadow of Death

One of the most difficult tasks we have as believers is to help bereaved people "digest" their sorrow and move back into their normal lives. Sometimes we have to deal with guilt ("I should have told her more often that I loved her"), family secrets, and even family conflicts. Where there's a will, there are relatives! Usually after four to six months, the bereaved ones are able to move out of the shadows and talk about the deceased without breaking down. The best sign of recovery is when the mourners remember funny things that happened in the past and can actually laugh about them.

Still, we never know when people will have "shadow moments," when in their imaginations they see the faces and hear the voices of departed loved ones. That's when they start to feel lonely and begin to remember and regret. A phone call, something in the newspaper, a song sung during a church service, or lunch in a favorite restaurant can without warning trigger memories and open emotional floodgates. They miss people they have loved and who have loved them, and they start to wonder when they will join them.

Parents who have buried little ones are especially susceptible to these shadow moments. Sometimes they fall into the "Little Boy Blue"* mode and leave everything in junior's room just as it was when he died. Having a "shadow room" in the home doesn't promote healing. Turning memories into museums embalms the emotions of the living and makes it difficult for hearts to grow and reach out to share as well as to receive. One of the best ways to honor the dead is to hug the living.

*"Little Boy Blue" is a poem by Eugene Field about the death of a little boy and how his room was left as it was. The little toy dog and the little toy soldier faithfully wait for the boy to return.

It's a mark of maturity to be able to process our memories and use them creatively in our lives and in the lives of others. James M. Barrie, author of *Peter Pan,* defined memory as God's gift to us "so that we might have roses in December." Yes, the roses will have thorns, but that doesn't keep us from enjoying their beauty and fragrance. Don't just see people in your memories; see God as well. He was there, of course, when it happened, and you can probably see His hand more clearly now than you could back then. Thank God for the memories, but don't linger in the shadow moments. Ask the Lord for some way to help someone you know make a good memory today.

David wrote about "the valley of the shadow of death" (Ps. 23:4). He knew that for the believer death is only a shadow. During his years as a fugitive and as a soldier on the battlefield, David knew there was only a step between him and death, yet he had no fear. To him, death was a shadow. We can't feel a shadow. We can't weigh it or capture it. Nevertheless, it's real to us, and it robs us of the light. But the light is there or the shadow wouldn't be there! God is with us when we walk through the valley experiences of life, and He's with us when we remember them and relive them in our minds. We have nothing to fear.

Blessed Are the Merciful

Jesus said that He came to "heal the brokenhearted" (Luke 4:18 KJV), and He uses His own people to help Him do the job. Our God is "the God of all comfort, who comforts us in all our troubles, so that we can comfort those in any trouble with the comfort we ourselves have received from God" (2 Cor. 1:3–4). Suffering in our lives not only encourages spiritual growth but it also equips us to minister to others who are hurting. The gifts of encouraging and showing mercy are greatly needed today (Rom. 12:8).

What should we do to help lonely people move out of the shadows and into the sunshine? What approach should we take?

1. Do a lot of listening. When passing through Shadow Valley, some people say very little while others seem to talk endlessly. Perhaps the latter need the sound of their own voice to encourage them, like the little boy whistling in the dark; but the former often speak with their silence. Every counselor knows that silence often says more than conversation and that constant speaking can be a subtle means of keeping certain topics at bay. Job's friends would have done more good if they had just sat silently for another week instead of lecturing him and bombarding him with questions. As you wait, pray that God will minister grace to the lonely person.

2. Listen with the heart, not just the ears. If we respond only to the person's words, we may get so analytical that we become judgmental and fail to hear the sobs of the soul. Don't reason people out of loneliness. Telling Grandma Perkins that she has family who visit her, friends who welcome her at church, and neighbors who greet her when she's outdoors may not compensate for the emptiness in her heart, because she misses a relative who is far away or a friend who is deceased. The wise listener responds not only to what people say but also to how people feel. Reflecting their feelings back to them assures them you understand, and that helps.

3. Apply the medicine of God's Word. "He sent forth his word and healed them" (Ps. 107:20). "The words I have spoken to you are spirit and they are life" (John 6:63). Don't preach sermons or give exhortations. Instead, carefully season the conversation with Scripture verses that declare the greatness of God, His love for His people, and His promise to be

110

with us in every circumstance of life. Perhaps the lonely person has a favorite Scripture you can read and talk about together. You might be able to sing a hymn together that's based on some favorite passage. And while you're doing this, pray for the Spirit to write the truth of His Word on the person's heart. Relate the truths of Scripture to the present situation and not to the past memories that may have triggered the feelings of loneliness. Listen to the memories but minister in the present tense.

4. *Pray together.* Sometimes I've turned a psalm into a personal prayer. You might pray individually and then close with the Lord's Prayer. When you pray, remember other people in the circle of friends and relatives and make it a "family" prayer. After the "Amen," it's good just to wait in silence and allow the Spirit to speak to the heart.

5. *Tarry long enough to tie up any ragged edges.* When the visit is about to end, a person sometimes will open up and ask a question or share a problem. Be flexible and be patient. One of the best ways to show love is to share your precious time with people.

6. *Promise to keep in touch.* A phone call helps, a friendly note can be read over again, and another visit is even better. Meanwhile, keep praying.

7. *Keep everything confidential.* Of course, if it's for the person's own good to tell a caregiver something, do so with great discretion lest the person lose confidence in your friendship.

"Blessed are the merciful, for they will be shown mercy" (Matt. 5:7).

Warren W. Wiersbe is Distinguished Professor of Preaching at Grand Rapids Baptist Seminary and has pastored churches in Indiana, Kentucky, and Illinois (Chicago's historic Moody Church). He is the author of more than 150 books, including *God Isn't in a Hurry, The Bumps Are What You Climb On,* and *The Bible Exposition Commentary: New Testament* (2 vols).